RIGID INFLATABLE BOATS

RIGID INFLATABLE BOATS

Colin Jones

WATERLINE

Published by Waterline Books
an imprint of Airlife Publishing Ltd
101 Longden Rd, Shrewsbury, England

ISBN 1 85310 313 6

A Sheerstrake production.

A CIP catalogue record of this book
is available from the British Library

Contents

Preface

This is a book for newcomers to the world of rigid hull inflatable boating and for all those friends who are already devoted to the breed. Equally, I should like to think that it will attract those who have 'just done a bit' of boating and who would now like to up-rate their level of adventure. My hope is that it will also be a refresher course for those whose driving and navigational skills are suffering the rustiness of disuse, but who would now like to catch up with modern hulls and modern accessories.

I wish them all as much pleasure in reading this book as I have derived from reliving past voyages, remembering diving expeditions, recalling days spent as a rescue boat, and thinking about old friends whilst I have been writing it.

Throughout the text, I have generally used the words HE and HIM to mean the masculine form and also its feminine equivalents SHE and HER. This writer's device has no sexist connotations, which would – anyway – be impossible on our own boat, where the co-skipper is a woman who completely shares the duties of boat handling and navigating and is invariably left on the surface to run the boat, whilst its other occupants grovel on the ocean bed, knowing that our RIB will always look after us whilst we are down and will always be right on station when we surface.

HE and HIM, therefore, are a writer's tool of convenience to avoid breaking up the text with repetitive HE OR SHE and even HE/SHE. In this, I have followed international and linguistic convention to improve the quality of the work and to maintain the ease of reading.

I wish you all the super boating activity which we have enjoyed as a couple and which we have shared with other RIB devotees of both sexes and all those other marvellous boating amateurs and professionals whom we have been privileged to meet en route from Here to There.

We raised a few eyebrows at Alderney

Chapter One

Introduction

The rigid hull inflatable boat is – arguably – the safest and most versatile inshore water vehicle of our time. Its application span covers the entire marine spectrum from the minuscule, three metre yacht tender right through to fifteen metre, ocean-going versions with cabins and enormously powerful twin inboard diesel engines. No other single type of vessel can claim such a panorama of employment. Nor has any other 'singleton' simultaneously found favour with The Royal Navy, The US Coastguard, military agencies, the North Sea oil industry, police, divers, off-shore racers, the RNLI and many other professional and leisure using owners.

Yet, nobody sat to a drawing board with the set intention of designing this marvellous piece of equipment as a conceptual, ab-initio marine project. The boat with the hard bottom and the soft top was not invented: but sort of evolved from a series of accidents, problems, solutions, necessities and some very sound seafaring imagination.

This haphazard arrival at the forefront of marine activity explains why the tangible product of all this experimentation and deep thought spent such a long time without a proper type-name. After all, a catamaran is a clearly defined entity and the same can be said for bilge keelers, ketches and others. Our subject, however, was variously dubbed Rigid Hull Inflatable (RHI), Semi-Rigid Boat, Searider and Sponson Hull Boat. Happily, terminology now seems to have settled on Rigid Inflatable Boat (RIB) and we shall follow current accepted practice, because it perfectly defines the combination.

This is a book about RIBs – all of them.

My own fascination with the breed began when I was asked to evaluate a 5 metre boat for a magazine report. It had been designed by a newcomer to the boating world and was to be built under the umbrella of a company which had previously only been interested in manufacturing in metal, so had neither experience of glass fibre lamination techniques, nor of the complex patterning and labour intensive cold adhesive methods needed to create an air retaining boat shape in malleable materials.

The project was rendered even more doubtful because the designer/builder was proposing to use a form of polyurethane (PU) for the inflatable part of the new craft, rather than the usual neoprene/Hypalon mixture. PU had always had a thoroughly bad reputation. It was mostly seen in playboats and very cheap inflatables, where it was dangerous because it had little resistance to abrasion and even less to tear. A pin-prick could rapidly become a long slit. Yet, because the price of this new boat which was delivered to our door on a wild March morning was high, the materials had to be very tough. A telephone call to the fabric supplier confirmed that not only was the new PU very strong, but a derivative made to a military specification that could be attacked with a knife and would still survive.

The sixteen foot boat had been delivered, complete with a three cylinder, 85 HP Yamaha outboard motor, which seemed to me to be far too much power. I could not have been more wrong. We took this new type of boat to sea that same day in spite of the wind and waves. It handled the power with ease, got onto the plane in a couple of seconds and not only stayed there without chine wobble, but was obviously bettering forty knots at 4500 RPM. Both in the short chop of the estuary and out in the swell beyond the bar, it behaved like a real seagoing thoroughbred. I felt safe and hooked, much to the consternation of my regular diving partner at that time, who is an airline pilot used to landing passenger jets at 200 mph. He was cowering in the bottom of the boat, whilst I happily threw it into corners and down surfing rollers.

CT, our first boat gave us some surprises

This relationship was strengthened on a visit to Swanage, where the Coastguard asked if I could go into the tidal maelstrom of Peveril Ledge, where a small dinghy had been swamped and its occupant been thrown into the water alongside. The man turned out to be twenty stone and both unathletic and uncooperative. Yet the boat behaved quite beautifully in the waves and the power to weight ratio was so fine that it could be held stationary in that six knot tide and manoeuvred gently up to the recalcitrant casualty. We could not heave his bulk into the boat so, when we had drifted into the calm of Durlston Bay, we managed to get a rope around his shoulders and another onto his legs and tied him off short to the internal bow eye and a cleat alongside the driver's seating console, where he was secure and well away from the propeller.

When we blasted the boat full ahead, she came onto the plane so quickly that our grumbling dinghy owner was automatically flopped up onto the tube and fell into the boat like a mass of swearing blubber. As rescue technique it was very unorthodox, but remains a huge compliment to the versatility and handling qualities of what, to me, was a completely new water vehicle concept at that time.

Those are two key words, which go a long way to explain why I have never lost my fascination with RIBs, nor ceased to learn new things about them. They are capable of most seagoing tasks and do them with style. In our twelve year association, I have used mine for diving, angling, lobster potting, yacht tender, rescue craft, guard boat and as a bed and breakfast cruiser.

The RIB makes a superb dive boat or cruiser

This last use is probably the ultimate accolade. A recent cruise from the South Coast to Tréguier in North Brittany is a good example. A normal cruising yacht, given fair wind, would expect to make the 125 mile crossing in about twenty four hours. Our small flotilla of RIBs made it in five hours, which gave plenty of time to walk up to the hotel and to enjoy a shower and a drink before dinner.

Other skippers in the marina were amazed and envious. None of our crew was ill en route and the navigation was – if anything – simpler than the same task on a five tonner. To the RIB enthusiast, such a cruise is nothing very much out of the ordinary. We regularly travel solo from our seaside home in Dorset to the Channel Isles and are never afraid of the weather.

The RIB will either cope, or we use its speed to run away from any weather whose looks we dislike.

These are just a few of the reasons why the prospect of writing a whole book about RIBs is as thrilling as it is daunting. There is so much that you can do with the RIB and once you own one you will never lose the thrill of opening up the throttle and of watching the nose rise a little until she climbs over the hump onto the plane, then shoots away flat, fast and level like an arrow from a well wielded bow.

There is so much to say about RIBs that the problems are not what to include, but what we must leave out. With such a vast subject, where to start? The beginning is not a bad place.

Chapter Two

History and Development

An Ugly Duckling Born By Accident

Trailer boating, in both the commercial and the leisure fields, has followed the evolutionary path of the wheel and come full circle. It has seen the available boats change from massive wooden constructions and large payload capacities to very light boats, which could be stuffed into the boot of the car, or shoved into a cockpit locker on a small cruising yacht, right up to the present, fascinating position which has currently settled about half way between the two. So, we are part way back to solidity again, but in a much modified form.

RIBs now come in all shapes and sizes

This curriculum vitae is a classic example of how the demands of progress perpetually create compromises to permit the best possible manufacturers' market target flexibility and the greatest possible number of buyers getting boats suitable to their intended use. Put very simply, you can have a highly portable boat, a super sea boat, an utter speed machine, or a tremendous load carrier, but you cannot have all these qualities in just one boat.

Having said that, the RIB comes closer to this universal perfection and application than just about any other water vehicle yet invented. Considering that there is a large amount of inflatable material used in its construction and that the term 'inflatable' appears in its name, it is not surprising that many people still do not differentiate between what is an ocean thoroughbred and the other sort of air filled boat, disparagingly known as the 'rubber duck' and often viewed with utter disdain and distrust by those who do not understand how they are built.

Fortunately, Modern RIBS are a very far cry from the evil smelling, leaky, blow-up 'doughnuts' invented to improve the mobility of Allied troops during Hitler's War. This super portability was subsequently seized on by divers as a way of being able to launch closer to good and often almost inaccessible dive sites. They chose this option partly because the world was then still lacking in slipways, but also as an alternative to long, bouncing, back-breaking journeys out to wrecks, whilst constantly being apprehensive about the era's abominably unreliable outboard motors.

Through the Nineteen Fifties, the inflatable boat developed along two completely separate paths. The first of these was created by much improved rubber technology, which gave better air retention and permitted the construction of inflatable keels and bigger boats. These hulls were a slight departure from traditional inflatables because the pneumatic keel gave them more of a boat shape, with a V going down into the water. They performed much better than the

The stern cones resist rearing up

'doughnuts'. Then, the development of inflated cones projecting beyond the stern of the boat, created additional fore and aft stability and permitted the use of larger, faster engines, mounted on an integral wooden transom.

Inevitably, inflatable boats began to get so big that nobody could be bothered to deflate them and they would certainly not fit into the boot of the normal, family car, so the big marine balloon on its own flatbed trailer initially became very much a part of the diving and exploration scene, then spread slowly to general pleasure users. Traditionalists still mocked them, but the aficionados took all the jokes in good humour because they could see the beginnings of a boat form which had come to stay.

The role of the Atlantic College

Path Two was almost certainly initiated by a department of Atlantic College in West Wales, where they were using inflatable boats as patrol craft for the dinghy sailing fleet and to give students search and rescue training. Because the boats were repeatedly hauled over the beach, the abrasion and general wear and tear, especially to the thinner and more vulnerable floor of the boat, was proving to be very expensive. The College workshop responded by bonding large sheets of thin plywood to the outside of the floor. Where this treatment was given to the boats which had an inflatable keel, or a stiffened full length wooden insert inside the hull (both giving a shallow V -shaped configuration) the pioneers found that they had accidentally created a boat which gave a much softer ride than the slamming, back-crunching, flat bottomed ordinary inflatable and it could also be driven much faster in waves.

The RIB rides a trailer with ease

It took several years of playing about with plywood before Atlantic, plus one or two others, finally got around to the logic of a complete, shaped, wooden under carriage, with normal tubes bonded onto the top. This was even more successful than the originators had foreseen, so it sent people scurrying about looking at the under water shape of hulls for combined speed and safety. This route inevitably led to the ideas of Don Shead and Ray Hunt, whose boats were renowned for their ability to maintain off-shore racing speeds, even in adverse conditions, without too much body shock for the crew, or becoming airborne off every wave, then bringing the outfit to a complete, slamming stop in every trough.

If the rigid hull inflatable was developed by accident, its popularity was soon boosted when the Royal Navy replaced their whalers with Avon Seariders and the RNLI commissioned an inshore lifeboat, commemoratively named The Atlantic 21. Again, sport divers were the first to see the possibilities, but even they took a bit of time to realise that as they were already trailering their boats and adding a variety of equipment, it made more sense to opt for a better shaped hull with a stronger construction.

The Avon Searider has stood the test of time

In these early days, it also has to be admitted that many people were deterred from ownership because the only available RIBs were prohibitively (and possibly unnecessarily) expensive and that this position was maintained by the total lack of market competition. The monopolists of the time were making vast profits from military and professional contracts, so tended to guard the mystique in order to retain their best markets at good financial levels.

By this time, the RIB had come to be seen as an entity in its own right, but still had no type name. Because the Avon Searider was by for the most successful model of these early days, almost all RIBs were called 'the searider' by those who did not understand them. Some purists objected and began to use the clumsy names mention in the previous chapter, but we were at this time at a stage where the RIB was sufficiently developed to have a definition.

For our purposes, the RIB is a boat which has a solid mono-hull, with a V shaped keel probably in GRP and is topped by an air-filled collar which accounts for at least fifty percent of the boat's volume and efficiency. The aberrations and attempted semi copies have no place in this work and – to be fair – most of them have not stood the test of time and market factors. There have been various attempts to put narrow inflatable collars onto speedboat and sailing dinghy hulls, but these hybrids have never been popular enough to merit a production line. Possibly the most far out concept has been the copying of the RIB shape in aluminium. This recognises, as the RIB does, that the tube is a very strong shape, but to have the weight of metal knocking against quays, other boats and the heads of sluggish divers and skiers, removes it entirely from the RIB concept of being virtually one long fender. These 'freaks' are not for us.

The RIB comes of age

The real breakthrough into modernity and popularity came in the late Seventies and was probably triggered into acceleration by Hull based designers Frank Roffey and David Haygreen (both sports divers) who both started producing boats which were as good as anything else on sale, but at about 50% of the price.

Since then, the RIB has become all things to all men and has just gone on and on growing both in numbers to be seen on the water and in the number of applications for its versatility. Its ability to carry loads at speed, its kindness to crew in waves and above all its utter safe, unsinkability have made it the first choice for uses almost without number. There are now many forms of RIB and many manufacturers, styles, construction methods and materials. It remains one of the fastest growth and development areas of the marine trade and this shows no sign of slowing.

There is currently plenty happening in the RIB World. The increasing number of water sport and ski owners are demanding more stylish colours than the traditional grey, black and orange and they are also developing seats and cuddies, which are concepts and additions a long way removed from the traditional, very practical sit-astride, jockey console. Much of the best tube material now comes from The Far East, where there are some interesting experiments being conducted with high frequency welding of rubber materials. In Europe, rubber fabric development seems more concerned with polyurethane and has developed one material which is almost totally indestructible by the elements and is exceptionally difficult to pierce, even when attacked with a sharp knife. In spite of this toughness, it still retains its ability to bounce off walls and other yachts without damage to itself or to the contact.

The RIB is also simultaneously growing and shrinking. In recent times, there have been passenger carrying monsters commissioned and also a whole host of small, davits carried yacht tenders, right down to 2.75 metres and less.

All this interest and activity means that the RIB is here to stay for a very wide span of civilian and military purposes. So, its versatility apart, what makes it such a good boat?

They even build them with cabins

Chapter Three

Handling the RIB at Sea

The adage that if something looks right, it probably is right certainly applies to most rigid inflatable boats. It could even be carried further into the philosophy that the properly set up RIB also feels right. It is the sort of boat which gives both the driver and his passengers enormous confidence because of the way it behaves.

You would best appreciate this by being in an engineless boat broadside on in big waves, or even in breaking surf. An alternative to being engineless would be to get some weight forward in order to trim the boat level, just as though she was up on the plane; ie you are balancing the boat just as she was meant to be – flat and level – not pulled down at the tail by engine weight at rest.

It heels in waves but is still quite safe

If the wave strikes the tube with any real force, the whole inflated element will probably flex slightly on its hinged attachments. This very slight inward rolling absorbs some of the impact. The boat then begins to list sideways as the wave gets underneath the tube and hull and will continue to heel over until the down wind, down hill tube is sufficiently immersed to be exerting its positive buoyancy up-thrust.

When this point is reached, the heeling stops, the roll stiffens and the whole boat moves sideways until the wave has passed beneath. Such lateral stability is only possible with the RIB's combination of light weight, flexibility and high buoyancy factors.

Party trick – full lock and full throttle

You also see this well when a driver performs the party trick of winding full lock on the wheel and opening up the throttle. The boat might heel over as much as 60° , but when it has reached its buoyancy datum point, it simply resists all further inclination and

21

goes on spinning like a top around its own axis. Even putting a passenger down on the lower tube does not have much effect on the angle. What generally happens is that the engine gives up before the boat and sends its prop spinning madly into aeration.

If a real mishap occurred, there is no danger that a well built RIB will sink. It is designed to support its rated payload of passengers, plus equipment, plus engine, plus swamping water. I have been aboard a 5.8 m RIB (which did not even have a sealed hull/floor chamber) whilst it was deliberately filled with water, but it still easily supported six divers, complete with cylinders, weight belts and all the other sundry ironmongery which the breed finds necessary to take down to the ocean floor.

Because the helmsman feels safe in the boat, he can drive it with confidence. The RIB is very much a driver's boat. I have never lost the shot of adrenalin which I always get when I take mine to sea, but also know that I must never take my eyes of what she is doing. The RIB is not a boat for slouches: she is much too lively. To get the most from her potential, she needs to be driven very positively and with plenty of throttle action.

The boat and motor partnership

When we talk about driving the RIB, we really mean driving the boat and the outboard motor, because the propeller plays a greater part than any other factor in controlling what happens to the boat. An outboard in neutral gear has very little turning effect on the hull even when it is gliding forward. To alter the boat's direction, you 'turn her on the prop', or 'drive into the corner'.

This is best appreciated when a novice driver is asked to make a 180° turn onto a reciprocal course – possibly to pick up something which has been dropped overboard. He will usually keep the engine revs high and constant, whilst trying to get the steering

At speed you go the long way around a curve

wheel onto full lock. When he has overcome the resistance of the propeller, the boat will go around in a very wide circle and will generally end up with the object to be retrieved still twenty to thirty metres off abeam on the inside of his curved path.

A much better way to get very quickly onto a reverse course is to cut the engine revs right back until the throttle- control lever is just short of the neutral position. Then, whilst the propeller is slowing, put on full lock, which is easier when the resistance of a fast spinning propeller is less, followed by opening the throttle as much as is necessary to get the rate of turn you require. This is using the RIB's best qualities of super lateral stability and high power to weight ratio, so that she spins like a top. In fact, on most occasions, you will need to start taking some wheel off, to avoid over shooting the reciprocal, just as soon as you 'give her the gun' again. If, for some reason, you must make your reciprocal turn at high engine revolutions, the RIB responds very well to the classic Williamson turn used by professional skippers to get onto the reverse line for anchoring, or in response to a man overboard alarm.

23

Driven on the prop, she spins like a top

To achieve a Williamson, the wheel is put over until the boat is
headed about 70° to 80° away from her original course. It is then
immediately put onto the opposite lock until the compass reads the
reciprocal. Generally, the boat will then be very close to running
back up its original line of travel.

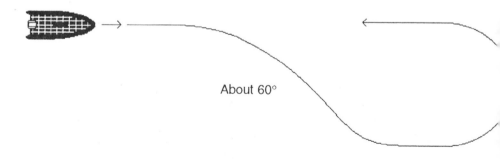

About 60°

The Williamson Turn

Before making either manoeuvre, the skipper should shout a warning to the passengers. The RIB turns so sharply by Method One that it is very easy accidentally to jettison a crew member over the side and even to put him at risk from the prop.

Equally, when making a high speed turn, the RIBs deep hull, with its V shape carried right back to the transom, grips the water very well. There is no appreciable tail skid, but the G forces will move the boat bodily sideways away from the centre of the turning circle. This drift is not dramatic and is usually accompanied with the boat still very flat. The problem arises when a contrary wave impedes the drift and the boat not only snatches, but kicks into a momentary list to the outside of the circle. At best, this is very uncomfortable. At worst it can actually jerk an unsuspecting passenger out over the tube.

The all important deep V

Coming alongside

This concept of always manoeuvring on the propeller is fundamental to good boat handling when coming alongside other vessels and quay walls. The acid test of a driver's skills will always be to ask him to put the boat alongside, and to get away again in any wind or waves.

Because the RIB is so light, she is very susceptible to gusts of wind. The remedy is to keep the boat moving positively through the water, with the prop turning – albeit slowly – for as long as possible. As soon as you put the gear shift into neutral, you have lost 95% of your ability to turn the boat's head and are at the mercy of the elements.

In the RIB, it is more than ever essential to follow the good seamanship practice of getting the boat lined up parallel to the berth from a good distance off. These coxswains who roar in at right angles to the wall, then kick the boat round parallel are only showing off to themselves. They risk denting both boat and ego.

By being on course from a long way out, you can approach at best speed, with the propeller keeping the boat nicely under your control and the helm just tweaked slightly and occasionally from amidships. You can then let the boat glide in neutral for those few feet which are essential to let the propeller pass clear of turbulent water. Then, a touch astern, with the blades gripping well in still water, will stop the boat without fuss.

However, life is not always this simple. If you have to approach a quay at an angle, try to avoid any sudden movements, or any abrupt changes of engine revs. The RIB tends to over-react to brutal throttle use and can create problems. The aim is to get in on a gentle, constant arc until it is time to shift into neutral. During the glide period, turn the wheel to get the helm into its central position. Then, when you kick astern to take the way off the boat, she will stop in a straight line.

To see why this, often ignored, centralisation is essential, you need to remember that propellers both push and pull. In the same way that a turn ahead is accomplished by the prop pushing the stern of the boat in the opposite direction, when spinning astern, the propeller pulls the boat towards itself.

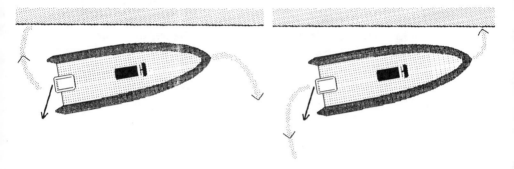

Right hand prop going ahead
pushes stern into quay

Reversed, it pulls stern out
and crashes nose in

A classic coxswain error is to come alongside with plenty of right hand wheel applied to turn the boat's nose away from the wall, whilst he watches the stern swing in. Then, when he goes hard astern to stop her, the bow is pulled hard back into the wall and the stern moves out in the classic and comical ostrich parking mode – head well in, tail well out.

Moving the RIB away from a quay wall is not generally a problem. The boat is usually light enough to be pushed bodily sideways. This apart, it is easier to come out slow astern than going ahead, for a number of reasons. The chief of these is that the tail swing in forward drive is exaggerated, so it is quite easy to clout the wall with the cones. Also, many RIBs have high tubes towards the bow, connoting high windage and occasional problems getting the bow to come round against it. Until you become very confident and able to use plenty of power safely in manoeuvring, the RIB is not the easiest boat to handle in tight corners. She does not carry her way like a traditional displacement boat when the engine is idling. On the other hand, the very fact that the RIB is built like one very long, very fat, very soft boat fender means that it rarely causes damage to itself, or to other craft.

Once you get the knack of combining wheel, wind and throttle, all the harbour problems disappear. Experienced drivers will get the boat into the tightest berths, no matter what the weather. The place to get this confidence and to practice coming up to buoys and other boats is outside the harbour, where there is plenty of room and rather fewer critical eyes. Anyway, it is out on the open sea that the rigid hull inflatable boat and powerful outboard really come into their own.

Driving the RIB at sea

On a flat, calm day, driving the RIB is very little different from piloting any other quick boat, except that the acceleration per horse power is greater. All RIBs are light and lively. To get the best performance you must have the boat properly trimmed, which means getting it to run in the attitude which it would adapt if left to its own devices on a pond. This is to say that the hull will float flat – horizontal even – with 90% of the tubes clear of the water.

The more quickly you can get on the plane, the better. As the engine is powered up, the stern of the boat is pulled down and a rolling wall of water builds up under the forefoot of the hull. Badly driven boats hang on the rear slope of the hump, where they remain with nose up, kicking up an unnecessary amount of wash, with the engine labouring, hunting and struggling. It is the RIB at its worst.

When you get it right, the boat only hangs for a couple of seconds, until that magic moment arrives and the bow drops and the RIB flies away flat, fast and level, almost as though she has suddenly

This one is struggling to get onto the plane

gained her freedom. This is one of the best part of RIB driving and
one which never ceases to give even the most experienced driver a
bit of an adrenalin buzz.

If the boat struggles to get onto the plane the causes might be one
of several.
[1] There is too much weight in the stern, so the widest part of the
boat is dragging and creating too much wetted area in the worst
possible place.
[2] The outfit is under-powered.
[3] An unsuitable propeller has been fitted. It might be too coarse in
pitch, or too large in diameter for the load which is being carried at
the time.

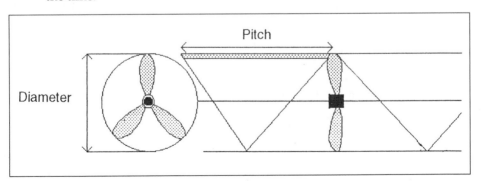

Because it is a light boat, the RIB will go fast even if it is badly set up and trimmed. There are many rigs with enormous engines on the transom and they really go, even if the driver is clueless. Typically, we have seen a 6 metre RIB with a 140 hp outboard being slaughtered for speed by an exactly similar boat pushed by a 90 hp 3 cylinder outboard. The winning combination was properly trimmed and – above all – had a propeller appropriate to the load.

When she is up and running she really flies

We shall return to this all important topic of props, but prudent owners have a couple of models in different configurations and change them according to circumstances.

Once the boat is up and going, the prop can be trimmed out a little, which will give a couple of knots more speed, or permit the cutting of engine revs to a more economical level. The trimming out needs to be done carefully because it decreases the amount of hull in the water and makes the steering lighter and more touchy. Most boats will have an increased tendency to pull to port when 'trimmed out'. If she gets into a skitterish chine wobble, trim back in a few degrees, or cut the revs.

Performance

The speed you will get on flat water is obviously determined by horse power and hull design – of which more anon. All boats have a maximum hull speed which they will not surpass, even with a bigger engine. In looking at performance, you should also remember the Square Law, which says that (roughly speaking) in order to double the speed, you need to quadruple the horsepower.

However, many RIBs are very similar, so the following mid range boat/engine performance figures below are a practical guide of what to expect. They are taken from one of our own boats – a 5.8 metre craft with two persons on board, powered by a 90 hp oil injection engine, swinging a 13.25 x 19 propeller.

At 4,000 RPM the boat cruises at 28-30 knots at 4 gallons per hour. Increasing the revs to 5,200 puts the speed to 35 knots and the fuel burn to 6 gph. The maximum hull speed we reckon to be about 50 knots (hairy) and we have actually achieved 38 knots with the 19" prop fitted.

Driving in waves

The first waves you meet are usually the wash from other boats. These will generally be relatively small and not be dangerous to the RIB's progress, so anything up to about a metre can almost be ignored, even at speed. You soon get the knack of either turning the boat so that you travel diagonally along them the troughs and crests, or of turning squarely in to take them at right angles. The aim is to stay in the waves for the shortest possible time. The head on approach gets it over quickly with a sharp, noisy bash, whilst the diagonal, sidling approach is more comfortable but still utilises the RIBs excellent combination of fore and aft plus lateral stability. You will appreciate this most when trying to make headway against wind and waves. Here we are entering a skill area where you really have to think about your driving.

RIBs best take waves diagonally

The primary essential is to get your eyes well ahead of the boat. Waves away from the shore do not follow a regular pattern of lines. The surface often seems to be made up of dozens of small waves, all moving in the same direction, but being steeper in some places than in others and sometimes having patches where the surface is flat enough for you to go from one crest to another, with no trough in between. It sometimes appears that you are on a small plateau.

The good driver will be constantly seeking out these flatter areas and altering course slightly to steer from one to the other, so that he can keep the boat moving at speed. From time to time he will also either speed up, or slow down a bit to get the boat to coincide with a smooth patch. This technique gets to be automatic with experience, but it must be done quite consciously until your eyes put you on autopilot.

The technique also tells you one other very important pilotage rule. A good RIB driver's hand is never very far away from the throttle lever. In waves, it is in constant use. This of course, means that you must be able to reach it and work it very easily from your normal driving position.

The wave pattern ahead is rarely regular – so zig zag

The driving position

How the helmsman is set to the wheel and throttle lever is largely
dictated by how the boat is built. If it has been fitted out as a sports
boat with seats thwartship across the beam, there is not much you
can do to protect yourself in head on waves. You just have to sit
there and let your spinal column take the pounding and hope that
the cushions ease some of the forces of impact. This is why the sit-
astride, jockey seat is so popular with RIB skippers. It lets you stand
up so that you can cushion all the jolts by flexing your knees, just
like a horse rider rising to the trot.

33

Most drivers prefer to stand

Most experienced RIB helmsmen prefer to stand up to drive in waves, not only for comfort, but also because it lets you look at the waves well ahead of the boat.

If they are any size, the worst way to take these is 'on the chin'. The RIB has plenty of forward buoyancy and is light on the front end, so it can easily be made to get airborne off the crest of a head on wave. Then a chain of clumsy events follows in sequence. The boat crashes into the trough, or into the front of the next wave and stops. Whilst flying, the propeller goes into over rev, develops aeration and will not grip the water after landing, so the engine continues to scream. When the propeller does get a grip, it has to overcome the inertia of a dead stopped boat and struggles to get it going again.

Then the whole bone crunching, stop-start nonsense begins all over again. It really is a common, but crazy way of driving. Luckily, it can be improved as soon as the driver sees that he can use the RIBs stability combination (already mentioned) to maintain his speed.

He must constantly be thinking "keep the boat in the water and keep it moving."

This can be effected by dropping the head of the boat slightly away from the big waves: attack them slightly diagonally to take the rise and the crest in front of the drive position, just about where the straight part of the tube begins to turn in towards the bow. We are talking here of approximately a 10° shift of course.

The boat can then be driven up the front of the wave and the revs pulled back just before the crest, allowing her to slip (sidle is a better word) slantwise over the top of the wave and to speed up again as gravity and a bit of power take her down again.

This process takes longer to read about than to execute and it soon becomes automatic – you get into a rhythm of driving the boat into the wave and easing off the power. In big waves, this diagonal approach means that you will travel more quickly up-wind against them than you will manage by trying to bash straight into such seas. You arrive at your destination via two legs, a bit like a tacking sailing boat. Such a route will also be more comfortable to your passengers, much kinder to your engine and will burn considerably less fuel than the straight line airborne, crashing, semi sub aqua straight line basher.

If the waves are very big, the RIB's high power to weight ratio once more comes advantageously into play. It has enough acceleration to stay in the trough just in front of a big breaking, curly one. You can run along the trough, or even go with it, until you reach a less vicious place, where it is more suitable to point the boat back on line and cross over the top. Sometimes you will need to speed up to get away from this breaking water and at others you will slow down to let it pass ahead of you. Both methods are possible not only because the RIB accelerates well, but also because it comes very rapidly off the plane – does not carry its way – when the revs are cut.

One of our own best recent RIB runs was from Guernsey up to Alderney with head wind over tail tide and a nasty little four to five feet chop against us. In a displacement boat, it would have been a very slow and uncomfortable ride. We, however, were able to trim the prop out a touch, pile on the power to a balance point and literally went from one crest to another without touching the narrow troughs between. The situation created a lot of noise on the bottom of the boat, but we were able to maintain about 25 knots, knowing that the crew would want to give up before the boat began to complain.

Is she safe?

People who are new to RIB driving are usually apprehensive that she might flip into a backward somersault if driven too enthusiastically into head waves. This has happened, but it is an extremely rare occurrence, probably in waves of Pacific surf proportions and was not so much the fault of the RIB as to the breaking top of the roller. We are talking of a wave so big that it would somersault any short boat which did not have enough length to resist and enough weight to smash through the wave top.

If the throttle man is a bit boisterous in head on waves, he can get the boat airborne at about an angle of 75° to the horizontal, off the crest. What then generally happens is that the climb runs out of steam, the boat reacts to the huge lump of metal on its transom, reverses its direction and drops straight back – engine first – into the water. In the beginning, we did this a number of times but we are now convinced diagonal sidlers.

However, even this needs treating with respect if you are out in the sort of waves that you ought not to be out in. The nastiest RIB accident of our own knowledge occurred when a heavy, twin engined, three man boat was driven so hard up and across a big wave that she barrel-rolled, a bit like a fighter pilot celebrating a dogfight victory.

Having said that, any driver has to work quite hard, or to do something extremely foolish, to capsize a RIB in head seas. They look more frightening and the progress appears to be more spectacular, but the RIB is (like any other boat) safer into the waves than surfing with them.

A real mover, so you never lose the thrill

Downwind and down waves

Running with big waves can be very exhilarating, but is also the RIB's most vulnerable angle. There have been a number of capsizes in big waves dead astern, or slightly on one quarter. Again, the best avoidance technique is get your eyes well ahead of the boat and to use her strengths to zip into those patches where the seas are less severe.

The most important thing in stern waves is to dominate them. You must be boss. Reciprocally, the very worst situation is to be in the grip of a big wave so that it is deciding your speed. You must never run at the same speed as the wave unless you are deliberately (and dangerously) playing surf riders. A good driver will always be going faster than the wave coming from behind, or going slower, so that it overtakes him.

Most tail-sea accidents have happened because a big wave has picked up the stern of the boat as it drives the whole hull forward. A point is reached where the very buoyant, inflatable nose is driven into the lower back of the wave in front. There it ceases to go either forward or down, but the stern continues to rise. Finally, the boat is almost balanced on its bow, like a pencil standing on its point, so it behaves similarly, rotates and crashes onto its back.

To avoid this, think of the boat as a sea-saw. When it accelerates from a slower speed, the bow rises. When the revs are cut and she drops off the plane, the bow also lifts. This means that by judicious use of the throttle, you can always be offering a high, protective bow to the wall of water in front of it.

If you are travelling fast and feel that you are about to dive into the back of the next wave, back off the engine power to create a higher bow, which will protect the boat as it climbs up the wave's back.

Reciprocally, if you are running on a lower RPM setting and can feel the overtaking wave driving you into the one ahead, have the courage to pile on the power for a moment, make a good high bow to support the forward end whilst you drive hard up the slope, but cut the power back before you reach its top.

Failure to reduce will either get the boat airborne, even going down wind or, more likely, she will go through the middle of wave number three so fast that a huge slick of water will be thrown up and come crashing into the boat from both sides at a point just in front of the driver.

This has caused a number of RIBs to become swamped. They do not sink, but just sit there full of water, too heavy for the engine to get the boat sufficiently on the plane to make the self bailers effective.

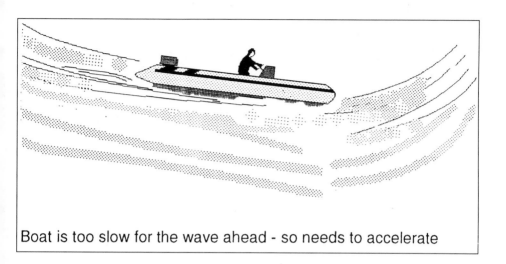

Boat is too slow for the wave ahead - so needs to accelerate

The saddest looking RIB we have ever seen belonged to a dive club, whose boat handler did just this about 100 metres off shore. Then the whole membership were only able to watch and grieve as the big waves took her into the beach, where she eventually broke up. Even though they had a dozen wet suited men in the water, they were unable to drain out the water-logged boat and neither were they able to pull its swamped weight and engine up the shingle.

This was a heavy price to pay for an act of stupidity. In the wrong hands, the RIB can be a very lethal weapon because of its power. In the right hands, it is arguably the most exciting, the most forgiving and the safest small water vehicle yet invented.

Chapter Four

The Hull

In the ensuing discussion of hull, shapes and materials, the main aim is to provide a prospective owner with sufficient information to be sure of getting the boat he really wants. There have been some very sad tales of people buying boats, then immediately regretting the purchase because the outfit was not fast enough for skiing, or it was too light to control a skier in a tight turn. There have been those whose new boat would not carry the envisaged weight and others whose families hated the 'wet' ride of a wide, shallow hull with fine tubes.

The hull is the basis of the boat and will decide many of the inflated tube parameters and will also play a big part in what the boat can actually be used for – its applications.

Physical construction

How the RIB hull is actually made and the type of materials used are now pretty standard from one manufacturer to another. The cocktail known as GRP (glass reinforced plastic) is almost universal in modern boat building and it is ideal for RIB hulls, which need lightness combined with strength. The most usual construction method is to apply coatings of resin to chopped strands of nylon, or similar material, randomly woven together to form a mat.

The use of thousands of strands running in random directions, increases the omni-directional strength. If the material was made with right angular warp and weft – like cloth – it would be prone to cracking along the lines and there would be some danger of several gaps coinciding into a weak area. The woven rovings, built up layer on layer and bonded by the resin, are immensely strong.

A few builders spray on the resin, but most RIB hulls are built by small, non-automated companies, who prefer to brush the resin in by hand. Greater thickness and added weight for increased strength can then be massively applied where it is most needed. Indeed, the common way of defining GRP strength is to quote that the resin has been applied at so many ounces per square foot.

This strength is most needed along the area of the keel, not only because this takes much of the impact when the boat lands from being airborne, but also to support the weight when the boat is beached (bad news for RIBs) and when a heavy boat is pulled up onto trailer rollers. Good builders also stiffen up a bit where the spray rails are likely to bear on trailer supports and put several extra layers in the place where a metal bow eye comes through the hull. The parts which you cannot see at first glance, but which are certainly worth asking about, is what is done to strengthen the points where internal, cross member bearings are installed and at the point where the transom is bonded to the sides and the deck.

This technology is very tried and trusted and has been around for long enough for any snags to be ironed out. It also has the virtue of being very resistant to blemish, but very simple to maintain and even to repair if the worst happens.

The addition of an inject of Kevlar and even of closed foam into the shape created by the GRP increases the strength by a very large factor but – unfortunately – Kevlar is currently so expensive that only a few rescue and military boat builders employ it.

Neither has aluminium found much favour in Europe, partly because the builders have no tradition of using the metal and also for reasons of cost. The one known attempt to duplicate the entire RIB shape – tubes and all – in aluminium would seem to have gone against most of the reasons why many of us are RIB devotees.

Hull shape

The actual configuration of the hull's shape will be the decider of
how the boat performs and how she can generally be used for
various tasks. Any discussion of shape naturally divides itself into
the contours and the characteristics of the exterior and the practical
configuration of the interior.

There are many variations on the deep V theme

Before discussing this in more depth, we should remind ourselves that most RIBs are a compromise. If you want a boat to go very fast, it must have a very good length to beam ratio. If stability is your main requirement, length has a large part to play, especially when the boat is moving, but at rest, the converse applies – beam betters length in proportion. Equally, a boat which must be driven hard in waves needs a deep V hull with the V running evenly along its length. You are here looking to a boat which has an entry fine enough not to slam to a stop (and to bruise the crew) every time it comes off the top of a wave. On the other hand, such a hull will need a number of modifications if it is to get onto the plane very quickly, especially if the power unit is small.

Equally, there are purchasers who are looking for a work boat with plenty of space and the capacity to carry a huge load. They also need a working platform which is very stable, but which, at the same time, gets them rapidly to and from the working site. Fish farmers, professional inshore fishermen and both commercial and sports divers are often in this category.

The wide body preferred by divers

The RIB can be made so that you can have absolutely all these qualities, but you could not have them all in the same boat. All RIBs are a compromise, not exactly a half way house, but having a shape which is emphasized towards the vessel's primary function. The general rough principle is that the more a hull is V shaped, the faster it will go. If it is to be a load carrier, it must be a flatter bottomed boat.

External shape

Compromise is achieved by varying the deadrise, which is the angle made by the bottom of the boat with a horizontal when viewed from ahead, or astern, along the line of the keel. A big load carrier might only have a few degrees deadrise, which would make her look flat bottomed. The opposite might be a ski racer RIB with 30° or even 50° of deadrise before a flatter hull section takes over.

Compromise means varying the deadrise

Because GRP construction methods are so versatile, many RIBs are made with a deep V, high deadrise, wave cutting angle forward, but progressively getting shallower to create a greater load bearing platform and to increase stability as it moves aft. This change from deep to shallow V can be infinitely varied and it can be made either very gradual, or very abrupt. It all depends on where the designer wishes to create internal space and how much payload he wishes to incorporate.

Racing boats and diving boats have differing deep V load-bearing parameters. It pays to look carefully and to try before you buy.

The exterior of most RIBs will also be graced with spray rails. These can either be small chines – alterations of angle – built into the actual hull, or are tailored from triangular extrusions on its outside. Their first purpose is to deflect the water close to the waterline well away from the boat. They help to clear a path for the hull to cut through, whilst also reducing that skin friction between hull and water. The less the skin friction, the less the wetted area causing drag, the faster and more economically the boat will run.

They also have the secondary, but still important, function giving the boat some lift when it is moving away from rest to climb over 'the hump' onto the plane.

The spray rails lift the boat and clear away the water

Some spray rails peter out after a few feet. Others go the whole length, in order to maximise planing speed assistance and generally giving the hull more support as it gets going. There is a discernible trend towards great experimentation with spray rails and chines and much copying of Scandinavian spray rail hooks and short, streamlined, vertical extrusions designed to break up skin friction and water surface tension.

Some builders who are very concerned with top end speed performance also incorporate a planing pad, made by flattening the very heel of the keel and slightly altering its angle so that it positively promotes lift and keeps the boat well up towards the surface of the water when she is going hard. The device works well, but there is a price to pay in increased slam in waves.

All this mini modification reinforces the idea that the design of spray rails, keel experiments etc is more a matter of trial, error and intuition than it is of precise mathematical formulae. The only really solid facts are that bad spray rails make no difference at all to performance, but good ones are an improvement. Happily, those RIB builders who use them in abundance have largely got it right. There are very few bad RIB hulls on the market.

This quality opinion is, of course, only confined to those traditionally configured, deep V, variable deadrise, monohulls. There have been various attempts to make catamaran RIBs and others with the so-call cathedral hull, comprising a fine bow with two inverted U tunnels on either side of the keel. The design supposedly gives better grip and stability and produces a water 'jet' effect.

The fact that none of these maverick boats has enjoyed a production run bettering a few models, is probably a more enlightened opinion than any which an author might offer. One reason for a failure to gain popularity is probably the spin-off effects which a changed exterior makes on the practical aspects of the interior.

The internal hull

Because there is not a vast difference between one RIB hull shape and its competitor's for our pennies in the same range, the internal configuration, seen against how we plan to use the boat, usually has the greater influence on deciding which boat we shall buy.

The major factor here will probably be whether the inside of the boat is fitted with
(1) a flat deck going across between the hulls and just below the bottom of the tubes, or
(2) the floor of the boat is a narrower 'plank' running centrally from stem to stern, with the sloping chine shapes visible inside the hull.

There are pros and cons to both.

The narrow floor

The narrow floor has the advantages that
(a) it is lighter and simpler to build
(b) it enhances the apparent freeboard
(c) it puts the crew safe and secure, well down inside the boat.
(d) if the boat has a sit-astride seat, the crew's feet can be comfortably braced against the sloping chines.

Its disadvantages are
(a) diminished flat working area
(b) the chines get wet and slippery, especially if you are wearing rubber soled boots, or dive fins
(c) it offers less bonding area to stiffen the transom to hull joints.

The wide flat floor

The wide flat floor can be braced by single fore and aft wooden stringer, or it can be supported on two rails for that part of its length which supports the most weight – eg seats and instrument consoles. The best construction is solid marine ply and other timber, covered with a coat of resin. One construction method even extends these longitudinal members and curves them up to makes transom knee braces. This makes a very strong, integral construction, ideal for larger outboard motors.

The flat deck has many plusses

Thwartship stringers are also necessary. The best of these are not simply put across as battens, but are shaped to the inside of the hull and 'glassed' into place with resin, so that they help to create several separate, extra buoyancy chambers.

This apart, the flat floor scores because
(a) it creates a very large flat working and load carrying space
(b) it makes a huge, extra buoyancy chamber
(c) it permits the installation of wide consoles
(d) it is kind to working and diving crew
(e) it protects the actual skin of the boat from dropped skis, weight belts and air cylinders
(f) it gives an extra bonding area to the transom joint.

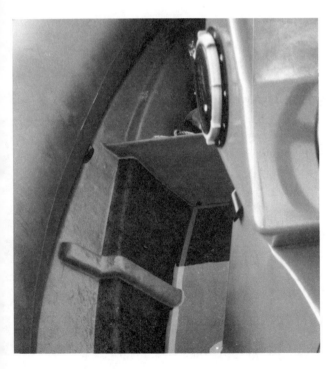

Solidly glassed in thwartship braces

The flat floor is disadvantaged because (a) it is more complex to install (b) it adds both weight and expense (c) it needs covering with a costly non-slip material (d) it puts the passengers and their weight higher in the boat where they are more vulnerable to wind and waves (e) any water coming in swills about over a wide area unless modifications are made to control and contain it.

Some manufacturers go for half way between virtually no floor and the full, sub-sponson flat deck. Others offer the option of a foam filled hull, which is fine for the first few years, but suffers badly if any water drips in via screw holes made for added equipment, or because the bow eye seating drips.

The flooding hull

Here would be an appropriate point not so much to write the obituary of the so-called flooding hull, but to point out that it really wrote its own. The theory promulgated in sales literature was that two holes in the bow of the boat would allow water to flood into the hull, thereby creating more stability whilst the boat was at rest. Similarly two holes in the transom would let the water out as the boat moved forward and got up onto the plane.

In practice, the system never worked as well as the sales hype promised, so many of us who bought these early boats, were so appalled at the time which they took to get onto the plane, especially when well loaded, that we blocked off the holes with tennis balls. It is interesting to observe that one manufacturer who used to praise the flooding hulls in its glossy brochure now offers an optional kit for sealing them up.

Another disadvantage of this sort of hull is the need to make sure that it is always free of water, otherwise residual dampness causes discolouration and encourages the growth of algae. This is even more a problem if you leave your boat afloat for any length of time

– say at a marina berth, or on a moorings whilst the parent boat is away at sea. The interior of such boats can get to resemble a marine jungle because it is an attractive place to weeds and molluscs. The smell which occurs when such a boat is brought ashore for servicing really defies description.

At the time of the flooding hull's introduction, the RIB was still going through its early development phase. Builders were still learning about this hybrid and made many experiments to balance out the hard and soft elements. It is certain that some of the early boats were made with the tubes too far from the waterline at rest. As soon as somebody stepped onto the tube to get in, the outfit gave a sudden, rolling twitch until the sponson hit the water. Flooding the hull stiffened the boat a bit, but it did nothing for its performance and was often a nuisance.

The tubes support the boat at rest

This brings us back to the point that a well built RIB will have some tube in the water and be very stable at rest, but will then ride on its hull alone when it is at its fastest.

Because the RIB was never specifically designed as a total, drawing board project, a number of such ideas have been tried and then slowly abandoned in the names of practical use, experiment, evolution and improvement. The methods of joining tube to hull are a good case in point.

The jaws effect

Early boats suffered a number of problems with tubes pulling away from the hard hull. This especially happened right up in the bows, where the effect of a huge, very buoyant area creates an enormous, up-lifting pressure every time the boat ploughs into a wave. 'Jaws' boats with a shark-like mouth opening at the front were all too common.

Since these bad old days there has been a very dramatic improve- ment in adhesives and in the complicated 'rubber' technology skills which boat builders need to create a nose cone, which is shaped to bond well onto a narrow part of the hull. They have also vastly improved the solid, GRP shelves and flanges on which the tube sits.

We shall discuss malleable materials more fully in the next section, so here suffice it to say that the hull's wing like protrusions (the best are curved to the shape of the tube they support) have been a difficult part of RIB construction, but most manufacturers deserve congratulations for the very effective way they have designed and devised solutions. A hull and tube separation of any magnitude is now a very rare occurrence.

The transom

That part of the boat on which we hang the outboard motor is the final element of the lower half. It has also had its past traumas, which were perhaps not surprising when you consider that we ask a narrow solid to air retainer joint not only to support a big engine, which might weigh anything up to 200 kg, but also to resist the enormous thrust which it develops. Then, when we make an emergency stop, we ask it to cling on against the tremendous pull of a high rev propeller going hard astern. Then there is the tremendous torque and twist effect of a 150 horses slamming the boat into a tight turn.

Excellent construction with fore and aft stringers glassed into the transom

Luckily, RIB designers have always been aware of the problem and have given plenty of thought to its solution. There are now very few poorly braced transoms on the market, but there remain a number of ways of creating the necessary support. The most common are:- (1) A pair of metal rods running from the transom to the floor of the boat and anchored by heavy duty bolts at each end. (2) Triangular wooden wedges, heavily glassed up and also screwed and glassed into the floor, the hull and the transom itself.

I will admit a personal preference for this second style, partly because the bolts can be dangerous to bare feet and the rods trap ropes and lines. The wooden wedges make life a bit difficult when you have to clean behind them, but they are very solid and strong and can be used as attachment points for a number of pieces of ancillary equipment.

Even a big engine is now not a transom problem

Transom height

The actual height of the transom is obviously dictated by the diameter of the tubes and the depth of the hull's V shape. This in turn decides the style of out board motor to be used. Some RIBs can accommodate a long shaft engine (which is generally standard on all horse power ratings above fifty) but some other boats need the extra reach of an 'ultra long' leg. Different engine suppliers have differing terminology here, so a bit of careful research is needed.

Water is inevitable

Sea water gets into the boat in a variety of ways. It begins when thoughtless, wet suited and booted passengers leap straight into the boat without a pause to let it drain off their absorbent garments. More comes in as spray on occasions and even more if the driver is too throttle happy going astern, or has not learned how to avoid being pooped by his own wake when he stops. Once in the boat, it flows up and down and goes from side to side so rapidly that even a couple of pints seems like a deluge. If you are kitted for skiing or diving it is merely uncomfortable, but if you are wearing ordinary shoes you cannot avoid wet feet.

The best solution I have seen was a small well right against the transom. The ingressed water flowed into it as soon as the boat moved forward and was safely contained there until it was pumped or sponged out later. One of my own boats was fitted with a small, submersible electric pump for this, whilst another actually had an 'elephant's trunk' type drainer installed in a fashion to keep its nozzle away from the propeller.

Self-bailers

Usually, however, the water catchment well is entirely independent of the tubular, or trunked self-bailers, which centrifuge water out of the boat just as soon as you get her going at moderate speed.

Again, a personal preference is for twin drainer tubes running out on either side of the engine leg. Yes, there is the logic that two balers will get the water out faster than one. However, the twins are most practical when the boat is badly trimmed either because the passengers are not well seated, or because half a dozen divers have just heaved in all their gear and are so busy discussing their adventures that they neglect to distribute it in balance.

The water they bring in, inevitably gathers on one side of the boat and can often be removed just by bringing one bailer into action. After all, the device is only made of a piece of four inch 'plastic' drainpipe inserted through the transom, to act as a solid attachment point for a tube made of sponson material and held in place by a stainless steel jubilee clip. Adding a second will scarcely break the bank.

Ski hooks

A couple of ski hooks on either side of the engine are also a good investment, even if you have no intention of trying to walk on water. They are ideal for holding a bridle which not only supports a tow rope clear of the engine propeller, but also means that any tow can be centralised. The RIB is not a good tug, so anything to help its performance is valuable.

On land, the ski hooks are a strong point used to rope the boat very firmly down onto the trailer and also serve to tie off the ends of the boat cover ropes.

This is one of the things I have most appreciated about the RIBs I have owned. They all have tremendous scope for customisation by adding your own personal touches. You can spend the Summer at sea and the Winter working in the garage to make a super hull even better.

Chapter Five

The Inflatable Tubes

Inflatable boat tubes still remain something of an apprehension and a bit of a mystery to those who do not know them well. Indeed, the malaise goes even deeper, because many yachtsmen who misuse and generally abuse their dinghies add to the poor reputation which air filled boats have in certain quarters. Such moans and groans should be part of history.

My own experience of traditional inflatables and RIBs now encompasses twenty years of using them for a variety of purposes from river running and angling via diving and yacht tendering to enjoying a number of foreign adventures with the RIB as a cruising boat in its own right. In that time, I have carried air boats both assembled and collapsed on the roof of the Land Rover, stuffed them into boat lockers, locked them in the caravan and heaved them around the open deck of our current motor sailer ketch where a couple of boats regularly get soaked during an annual three month trip down across Biscay.

Even in the mid beginning, back in the Seventies, tubes had certainly come a long way from their origins. They were no longer perpetually leaky and floppy. Most manufacturers had developed better materials and vastly improved adhesives. They had also learned much about joins and putting on seam tapes. If my early boat tubes gave trouble it was generally to the stress areas of the complex piecing and shaping to make the bow and at the caps to the stern cones, or where the tube abutted onto the wooden transom.

Since the early Eighties, however, I have ceased to worry about tubes. In a typical busy year, my own RIB is launched and hammered about a hundred times a year for a variety of purposes.

In all that time, I have never had a puncture and never had any problem other than air wicking out through an abrasion mark and a small leak via a sticky valve. Both were soon put right.

In spite of their soft, light appearance, boats made of modern air-filled materials are just as tough and reliable as those made of GRP and wood. They are now very long lasting and very proof against their environment. They do not suffer problems of splintering, cracking and osmosis and their air retention powers are phenomenal. My present boat gets its chambers topped up about twice a year – generally when the weather is cold and the air inside them contracts. This confidence is obviously shared by many professional and military bodies who not only see the safety virtues of the RIB but also appreciate the fact that in contact with walls and other boats it does not damage itself.

Tube development

Some RIB devotees get quite angry when the uninformed refer to their expensive boats as 'the rubber duck'. Not only is the term a bit derogatory, but it is entirely uninformed. There is very little rubber used in modern boat construction.

Inflatable tubes have evolved (and continue to evolve) in two slightly separate directions. One path has been followed by boat building outfits set up as off-shoots of tyre companies. They tend to employ materials and techniques which are part of their history and their greatest competence and they often have machinery and expertise which can be harnessed to boat building. The other path is followed by companies moving away from such older elastomers as neoprene and Hypalon™ and into polymers and polyurethanes.

The air retaining materials developed by both have differences and similarities. They follow different paths, but they have the same destination – which is a fabric with very high air retention properties, as well as being relatively simple to use in a variety of temperature and humidity conditions. They resultant tubes must be tolerant of extremes of heat and cold, resistant to puncture, tear and abrasion and should also have a high rejection of damage caused by salt, water, ozone, ultra violet light, carburants and discolouration.

The solution to this posed conundrum is now almost universally some type of fluid substance coated onto a mesh woven from nylon or polyester. Most manufacturers continue to use a cocktail of neoprene and Dupont Hypalon for their tube material. It is a well proven air holder and can either be coated on one or both sides of the mesh. An even better method is to 'calender' the viscous parts into the mesh, by passing all three elements of the ensemble through heavy rollers, so that the result is a comprehensive unity in which delamination, or separation of 'rubber' from nylon is almost impossible.

This process demands some very heavy investment in special machinery, but the big companies who make their own inflatable material have been prepared to make it. The remaining small to medium European RIB builders either buy from the giants, or they import from The Far East.

Small RIB has tubes of Oriental origin, but they are as tough as anything coming out of the West

This region has not enjoyed the best reputation for the quality of some of its manufactured goods, but tube material is an exception to prove the rule. Many Far East tubes and materials are as good as those produced in The Occident.

The reasons are historical and modern. A number of Oriental countries have a good tradition of work with rubber type substances and they have very sympathetic climates. They are also a very new industry as far as building boats is concerned, so they took the trouble to visit Europe before setting up. In this way, they avoided many of the weaknesses still present in Western work and manufacturing processes and were able to develop new machinery and improved skills of their own – high frequency welding is a good example.

The supply chain has now reached a stage where some of the best boats and materials for tubes come from Oriental countries and some well known boat building names closer to Greenwich obtain their elastomers from them.

Polyurethanes appeared on the RIB market after 1983 as a combined effort between a Manchester producer and a Humberside RIB builder. This was an act of some courage because PUs had previously been a serious boating disaster. The material was much favoured by the sort of playboat obtained from garage forecourts and seaside bazaars. It was thin and weak and a small compass point prick could quickly become a gash long enough to cause instant deflation.

This just does not happen to serious polyurethane which, like its more rubberised cousin, is set into a mesh. In appearance it is shinier and looks harder than neoprene-Hypalon, but it is very hard wearing. Boat tube PUs have obviously been inspected and passed to the relevant BSI requirements and PU boats have been in use with The Royal Navy, the military, rescue services, customs departments and thousands of divers for a number of years now.

My own experiments on PU off-cuts has shown that one advantage of PU is that small holes can be smoothed back to air tightness with a moderately hot iron and that larger damage can be made good without a buffing operation. I am not able to confirm this by any work on an actual boat because, even though I have been using PU boats since they were first available, I have not suffered any damage or inconvenience enabling me to put the experiments to the test of reality. My present PU RIB has an outer cladding of special, high specification material which can be attacked with a knife and it still holds together.

This is not to claim any superiority for PU as opposed to neoprene-Hypalon. (The military spec cladding was very expensive.) I have had excellent boats of both and have no real preference. It does, however, say that you can now buy boats in polyurethane materials without feeling inferior, or at risk.

Some of the best boats are now made of polyurethanes

Tube construction

The most common reason given for the high price of rigid hull
inflatable boats is that there is no good way to mass produce the
tubes. This is still a very precise, hands-on process, entirely done by
humans. It requires patience and dexterity and can only be done
one piece at a time. Each segment of the tube ensemble must be
made into a roll, bonded and given time to dry and cure before the
next operation can be performed. This takes time and money.

Once the lengths of rolled tube are made up, they may then be
double bonded again on both sides and interior and exterior seam
tapes added to complete the integrity of the air retention and to
protect the joint itself.

A common equation is that one roll equals one chamber, so that a
flexible baffle can be inserted into the tube. Having several
chambers obviously makes for a safer boat, with the baffle
inhibiting the transference of air from one to another.

Each chamber (or pair of chambers)is inflated via a simple valve,
comprising a seat with a centrally mounted rubber flange on the
inside. This flexes inwards when air is driven in from the inflator,
then compressed into a seal against the baffle by air pressure from
inside. This is an old and simple air retention device made into a
really first class product by modern manufacturing techniques.
Once the current generation of valves, with their snug fitting
covers, has been installed, you can generally forget about them. The
pressure relief system is also excellent. Not since about 1970 have I
received any report of a tube being damaged by over inflation
(Even that one was done by a clown with a dive cylinder and DIY
adaptor) or of one opening up because the sun caused such an air
expansion that the tube burst.

Attachment

It obviously takes many man hours to make up the complete, air filled top section of a RIB and to test it for leaks before the whole, elongated doughnut is dropped onto the flanges either sticking out from the sides of the hull, or protruding externally and internally on either side of the top edge. Again, builders differ in how they make their surfaces to support the tubes. There are some who opt for a foot of flange every two feet or so, which leaves a bit of manoeuvring room if the tubes are a fraction out. The more courageous – (dare one say the best) – are so sure of their tube construction skills that they build a very shallow trough right around the hull, give it a lick of adhesive and nestle the inflated tubes straight down into its support.

A variation of this method is to make the fabric hinges larger and to bend them across the top of the GRP flange. The main tube ensemble is then attached to them in such a way that there is not any adhesed contact between the air filled portion and the GRP section.

No matter which of the excellent attachment methods is employed, this long, double sided tube to hull joint is then usually finished off with a flange of boat material from tube to hull both inside the boat and out. This makes a joint which is simultaneously very strong and very watertight, but which still retains a bit of pliability. The tube can still flex and roll a little to absorb the shock of impact and to protect itself from crash damage against quay walls.

This sort of join technology sounds very simple,but is very long winded and labour intensive to put together, but it has one very important virtue. It works. It has stood up to everything from crossing The Atlantic, via North Sea rescue duty in Winter, drug enforcement chases in America and having thousands of heavyweight divers and their gear bounce it and bang it both on the sea and on land.

Tubes are bonded to flanges, then firmed up with hinges and tapes

Unfortunately, the same cannot be said of various other methods of attaching soft tops to hard bottoms. There have been zips and a number of eye and toggle methods. At one time, a major manufacturer made great play of tubes which slid onto the boat with a rubber extrusion running along a groove. Perhaps the best commentary on all these innovations and experiments is that they bided their hour, were tried out by the patrons and never reached the popularity of more conventional RIB building systems.

Some manufacturers like to change shapes and experiment with different tube to hull fixings

The sea is a very tough place, one of the big problems about easily foldable and removable equipment is that it very often does these things of its own volition and at very inconvenient moments. KISS – keep it simple, stupid, is very much part of RIB building efficiency.

Tube to transom

The final attachment task is to fit the inflated tubes into the transom. Here, the method of making the joint has scarcely changed since the early days of, so-called, sports boat inflatables, which were the first to utilise a wooden transom and projecting cones. After all, there are not many possibilities for the invention of new solutions to the problem of attaching a curved, air filled balloon to the edge of a piece of wood.

Early joints in this area were a weakness, even as late as when the first RIBs came along. The method remains one whereby the wooden section is cut to the size and shape of the tube's circumference and the two offered up with adhesive. A flange of material is then put inside and out to complete the join. It is here that the improvement has taken place. There are now some excellent, strong, thin, workable flange materials available and the current range of adhesives is so strong that the glassed up wood might even split before the joint's own hold gives way.

The compliment is that RIB transoms have been fitted with twin 200 hp outboard motors and have come unscathed through some very rigourous off-shore racing adventures.

So, we go out through that same door as in we came, with the message that air filled tubes are as tough as any other boat building material and are very reliable. This also explains why the double tube of fifteen years ago (one inflated chamber inside another) is a thing of the past. If this belt and braces security was needed, it is a safe bet that the RNLI and US Customs RIBs would be clamouring to have it.

The stern cones are now coming in for some extra design and improvement attention. These are flatter than most.

Tube diameter

From a purely theoretical point of view, the diameter of RIB tubes is not a clearly defined factor. Talk to designers and they will generally say that the "tubes do not need to be any bigger than they have to be." This is another way of saying "It all depends".

If you bear in mind the fact that the tubes of a well balanced RIB in full flight do not touch the water and that it will stay afloat even with all chambers deflated, it becomes obvious that – yes – they have a flotation and buoyancy functions, but they also do other things.

The first of these is to provide stability. When a person steps from yacht to tender, or from quay to RIB and kitted divers are coming in over the side, it is the tube which supports the weight. After an initial wobble, the RIB becomes very stable in all these situations. Academically, it only needs to be big enough to cope with the expected loads.

My first boat had narrow tubes, but was still a dry ride

The second function is to keep water out of the boat and off the passengers. If you are prepared to put up with a wet ride and the occasional swamped boat, you could build a perfectly usable boat having tubes of no more than 9″ diameter. There have indeed been some circuit racing boats designed down to this size.

Thirdly, the tubes protect the crew. They form a barrier which keeps them safe. Tubes mean that in big waves, or in tight turns,

You feel very safe in boats with massive tubes

the passengers are more secure because they sit 'in' the boat rather than 'on' it. The tubes create the well plus its topsides and provide the freeboard.

In all but a few sports boats with thwartship benches, the RIB's tubes are also an essential part of its seating and accommodation. So, if you are going to sit on the tubes for a longish passage, how high do they need to be so that you can get your legs under you for extra support and to keep your feet away from the crew members opposite?

In my own boat, I spend 90% of my driving and passenger time standing up, because this is the best way to cope with accelerative G forces and to cope with waves. If we have so many people on board that I cannot get two hands onto a stainless steel rail, when I am riding shotgun as opposed to steering, the inboard hand goes onto the rail and the outboard hand seeks out a tube mounted rubber grab handle. If the tube is of small diameter, this causes you to stoop into a back aching, muscularly inefficient position.

The inevitable compromise

As with all things maritime, eventual choice of tubes is a compromise. A boat with a very high bow and large diameter sponsons will give a very dry ride, but it may have a frightening amount of lift in waves and be difficult to manoeuvre in wind. Boats with narrow tubes are always wet.

In buying, you can generally be guided by a combination of the builder's advice and your own reactions. Most builders are RIB enthusiasts and users. My diving companion prefers sporty boats in bright colours, with thinnish tubes that make for easy re-entry into the boat after a dive. My own preference is for very chunky, large diameter tubes because they look more workmanlike. My present boat is a 5.8 metre model with 20" (51 cm) tubes. This is a compromise suggested by the builder, but it has worked well.

About 5.8 metres with 20" tubes is a popular combination

In choosing, you must also have a look at where the tubes are put onto the hull. Very big tubes diminish the boat's internal beam and reduce the space, so some manufacturers set the tubes well out on the flanges. This has made at least one boat too wide for legal, private towing. It just needs watching and sitting in. Personally, I would never buy a RIB unless I had ridden it at sea to get the feel of how it behaves in the sort of tasks I have in mind for it.

The optional extras

All RIBs come with a certain number of extra fittings, but the owner will usually want more. We shall discuss consoles and electronics later, but for the moment let us think of the things which are actually bonded onto the inflated section.

Grab handles

These have two functions. In primary mode they serve to give passengers sitting on the tubes something to hold onto for safety. Sizes are pretty much standard, because there are so few manufacturers and their products are ergonomically efficient. They work.

You must, however, sit on the boat of your choice, preferably on the water, to visualise your passenger distribution. There will be places in the boat where a seated crew member can hold onto a console rail and one rubber handle – just forward of the driver, for instance and opposite the rear end of a two person jockey seat. The handles must be placed for effect and comfort.

Further aft and in the very centre of the boat, people might be using two rubber hand holds, so they must be spaced accordingly. At the same time, think of skiers, swimmers and divers coming back into the bat from the water. They need handles sufficiently far apart to create a good leverage.

One boat we tried had the rubber grips bonded onto the tubes well down inside the boat. The theory was to keep an uncluttered top, to be at the correct place for an extended arm for anybody riding the tubes and to help get divers further into the boat.

Grab handle locations should be customised to suit different needs

They were a disaster. They constantly snagged ropes and dive hoses and created a vast amount of blue language from people getting even bluer bruises on their shins as they moved about the boat. Tall passengers got back ache from using them and shorter crew members could not hold them and sit on the top of the tube at the same time. Worst of all, the divers could not see them from the water and found it difficult to grab them when they could.

The proper place for rubber hand holds is up on top of the tubes, where they also best fulfil their secondary function of a grip point, when you are helping the winch man to get the boat onto the trailer. You also use them when you are manoeuvring boat and trailer around the boat park. Their position needs to be decided by both usages.

Lifelines

Lifelines fall into the same category,. The one boat I have used with them fitted internally was not a success. Passengers did not use them and diving friends tied off so many cylinders and bottles to them that they quickly became tatty.

The fashion for lifelines is to have a series of ship's lifeboat style loops down along the entire length. This works well, but the loops tend to splash and bang on the water at medium speeds. Some builders lace these loops through a thin rubber collar sitting on top of the tube. This is not a complete success. I have a good track record for pulling out the eyes of such arrangements, even in the normal course of handling the boat on shore. For a dry suit diver, who is likely to have a suit inflation valve in the middle of the suit's chest, they are a real snagger as he comes in over the side and a hazard to spare demand valves and instrument consoles when he is going out over.

Ship's lifeboat style lifelines are popular for some reason which has more to do with history than with efficiency

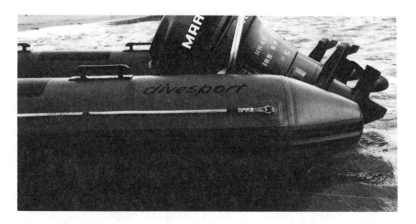

The taut lifeline is neat and efficient

A very seamanlike alternative is a fairly taut rope running from near bow to near stern just above the tube's exterior central line. Its very firmness gives divers and skiers a great feeling of confidence when they are hanging onto it from the water. You do not feel that the boat is drifting away from you.

Such a rope is also a good tie point for shore lines and shackle cords to take weight belts etc. It looks very neat in its adhesed loops and is absolutely invaluable for pulling and heaving the boat about on the land.

Double skins

A second layer of material at the place where divers come in and out of the boat, makes a lot of sense if the boat is to be used very hard or it is to be worked commercially. In normal, non club duty, it should not be necessary. Most boat materials will withstand at least ten years normal family wear and tear.

My present boat has a very expensive, very tough second skin over most of the outside of the tubes. It is very safe and almost indestructible, but for my own leisure purposes it has been a rather unnecessary investment. The boat in its raw form is plenty tough enough, so the money could have been spent on an echo sounder.

Rubbing strake

A good rubbing strake is absolutely essential. It comes in one of two forms. Some manufacturers simply put on a plasticised, rubberised strip about half an inch thick and four inches wide. This is fine as far as it goes. The alternative is a proper, fender style extrusion which stands a good inch clear of the boat's widest point. It looks tough and is tough.

Solid rubbing strake enhances the RIB's reputation as one long fender

The choice is caveat emptor. You get what you pay for. I would always be prepared to pay extra for the better protection, but that is why I am a devotee of RIBs. In spite of being filled with air, they look tough and they are tough.

Chapter Six

Inside the Boat

The RIB's interior is almost an embarrassment of riches when it comes to deciding on a lay-out. Because of the boat's versatility and stability, the new owner has the pleasure of a multiplicity of possible seating and installation but has, at the same time, the peril of being spoilt for choice. Planning the lay-out gets to be difficult.

As in so many RIB matters, we come back to compromise. You must make a decision about what is to be your prime use of the boat, then weight the compromise towards it. All else fits around the main purpose, which will also be influenced by the number of people you intend to participate in the activity.

A family boat cum water-skier will obviously look to four seats, with at least one facing astern so that the observer can watch the skier. A dive taxi needs plenty of room for the divers to get kitted up and a very clear space for all the equipment, which always takes up more room when they all pile back in after the dive. Equally, divers are not too concerned with having a seat for everybody. A club rescue boat, on the other hand, will be idling around on patrol for two or three hours at a stretch, so it needs two seats for the crew. A small RIB used as a yacht tender might not need seats at all.

So, arranging the interior is one of the fun parts of RIB ownership, but it can run away with the money. We shall talk about purchasing in a later chapter, but right here, we should counsel care in reading the brochures. Some manufacturers price up a complete boat, whilst others count seats, lockers etc as extras. This knowledge becomes even more important when you are discussing the value of a second-hand deal.

The family sportsboat

The RIB will never be a very major part of the competition club ski scene, but it is increasingly used as a dual purpose tug and runabout vehicle. Because most RIB builders are small companies, about 90% of new boats have a high degree of customising, ie they have been built to the client's instructions. They will all provide the sort of seating which you require but, generally speaking, the bigger companies do it better when it comes to thwartship and bucket seats. These specialists already have the seats made up in house, with a choice of colours. Installation of a double bench seat (two facing aft) is a simple operation for them, so they can keep the costs down.

An alternative is a bench seat for the driver and co-pilot, with a pair of bucket, swivel seats for the after passengers. These can be swivelled to face in either direction, both for view and comfort and also to help to trim the boat.

It is not part of our brief to point you towards particulars builders. Suffice it to say that there are a few companies offering a sports boat seating option. They also usually make boats in colours other than those traditionally associated with Search and Rescue. Look at the brochures. If a builder is aiming at the ski and runabout market, his catalogue will contain a picture of a brightly coloured boat – generally graced with what he considers to be a dazzling girl.

The ubiquitous astride

The sit astride seat, in various guises, is very much the RIB norm, but rather than just accept this as boat builder's whim, it is worth asking ourselves "Why?"

RIBs and RIB owners have been very much influenced by the rescue services. Early leisure users almost always had an admiration for the RNLI Atlantic 21 and the very powerful boats serving the North Sea oil industry. There was a certain amount of 'posing' in the air – a wish to be thought of as on the same plane as the rescuers and the professionals. There is still an amount of this in the air – with RIB crews wearing drysuits and white helmets with boom microphones, even when they are out for a smooth water jolly in a VHF dead area.

There has also been a more practical wave which recognises that such bodies as the RNLI have done a vast amount of research into seating and crew safety, but that not all of it is applicable to leisure craft. The result of this has been that the sit astride seat is by far the most common RIB crew accommodation – and there are some very good reasons for this choice.

The RIB is a very lively boat. When it accelerates hard, it takes on a pronounced slope towards the stern and getting it airborne is very easy. This performance has its up-side, but there is also a down-side that the crew could be thrown about the boat, or even right out of it, unless there is a means of helping them to stay in one place.

The RIB is also very hard on the lower back. Even if you are sitting on the pneumatic comfort of an air filled sponson tube, the spine takes the impact when the boat crashes back into the trough.

One more version of the ubiquitous astride seat   *Wise passengers stand up when it gets rough*

78

The result of this is that experienced RIB drivers and passengers very rarely sit down for any length of time. When the boat is being accelerated hard from rest, an unprepared passenger can be slid sideways along the tube. So, there is a natural reaction to lean forward to counteract the thrust. This is much easier to do whilst standing.

We have had some very uncomfortable passengers when they have insisted on remaining seated for a run in waves. Some come back several days later, still complaining of back ache and anyone with a spinal problem could do himself real damage. All these ills and groans vanish in a trice just as soon as we persuade our passengers to stand up, get a good handhold, then to stay relaxed on slightly bent knees like a dodging and weaving boxer, or to try to absorb the impact of waves by flexing the knees to catch the body weight in a water-borne copy of the horse rider rising to the trot, or a gymnast landing from a height.

In the case of the driver, it is much simpler for him to attain this standing position very quickly from a sit astride seat (often called a jockey seat) than from any other sedentary position.

This process of alternatively sitting and standing soon becomes absolutely automatic, as a sort of sixth sense builds up about when the wave effect is going to be at its worst and when it will be so slight that you need not bother. In fact, 'standing' is possibly the wrong word. More often it is more a case of taking your weight on your feet by raising your seat a couple inches clear of the bench. In this way, the impact of the hull either hitting a wave, or of dropping back into the trough, is absorbed by a flexible knee joint, rather than by a vertically inflexible pile of vertebrae and discs.

Watch your shape

The jockey seat is normally an integral part of a total console, but let us see it on its own for a moment. Over the years, it has developed from being purely a seat mounted on four legs with a clear space beneath to having a variety of other uses. Some of these have tended to detract from its prime function – somewhere to park the seat of your wetsuit in quiet periods.

The very early seats were unquestionably too low. They were built just high enough for a couple of standard five gallon outboard motor fuel tanks to sit beneath. This had the virtue of putting the occupants good and safe down in the bowels of the boat, but the drawback that the driver had to sit with his legs stretched well out in front of him. Short leg pilots could just about get a flat sole on the floor, but the point of contact for tall drivers was the heel. Anything else was either too gymnastic, or it entangled the knees with the engine controls.

This position was never very comfortable and not particularly safe either for balancing yourself laterally, or for shock absorption. There were a number of bruised spines both amongst amateurs and professionals. This so worried some commercial and Search and Rescue organisations that they put an upper age limit of forty years on crews. This was probably the wrong approach to the problem.

Inevitably, jockey seats got to be taller and the trend was to make them enclosed. Some designers began to see the sales attraction of a

A very low seat is not a good idea, but is sometimes unavoidable

dry storage space (always in short supply on a RIB) so began to think more of volume than of driver usage.

At about the same time, a whole rash of new boat builders came on the scene. They were looking for speed of construction, economics and – it has to be admitted – some also needed short cuts to make up for their lack of plug making engineering expertise. Their seats were coffin shaped boxes, the same width the whole way up and topped by a mass produced, oblong cushion squab. This gave more stowage and easy access for stowed gear, but also caused a number of bruised insides of knees and thighs.

Practically speaking, the best RIB seat I have ever ridden is of a height comfortable for the driver's ankle to crotch length. It starts wide, but slopes in and gets narrower towards the top. The cushion should be slightly dome shaped – curved across its width. This narrow, rounded format packs in more cushioning material and allows he important part of the seat to mould itself to the occupant's contours.

Unfortunately, such a seat is more time consuming and more expensive to make, but from the crew's point of view is much the most comfortable and the most efficient configuration yet devised.

A good seat should be contoured into a semi domed top

The passenger grips the metal rail at the back of the console

Handles and footles

When the going gets rough, the driver stays secure partly by balance and partly by leverage against the steering wheel. If the astride seat is a two person model, the rear passenger needs not only a back rest, but also a convenient hand hold. The best and most common solution is a U shaped stainless steel frame bolted to the rear end of the double seat. The passenger can use its back rest, whilst the tubing below is within reach of his hands, even when he stands up, either for a big wave, or because the driver stands and you can only get a view ahead by doing likewise.

There are two schools of thought about whether to include loops of material bonded to the floor to take the feet of driver and navigator. The theory is that the foot is inserted into the stirrup-like loop, which serves to anchor the user in the boat. The theory undoubtedly transfers into practice for some people.

Well designed passenger hand holds should be a feature of the seating console

There are also other practical considerations to these – so called – footles, which is a name to parallel handles. Firstly, they are a thorough nuisance when you are just moving about the boat and even more of a hazard to the feet and safety of inexperienced passengers. They are also an inconvenience when you are cleaning the boat's interior. In many hundreds of hours at the wheel of a RIB used in a variety of amateur, professional and Search and Rescue applications, even in atrocious weather, I have never felt any real need to have my feet constrained.

Indeed, the foot freedom can itself be a safety factor. There have certainly been a number of occasions when my own security was enhanced and my balance restored because I was able to move a foot very quickly to catch my toppling weight. Much as you do when you trip or stumble. I have also suffered top of the foot bruising from toe straps, but the final contra factor was undoubtedly going to the rescue of a diver who had broken an ankle. The poor chap had been thrown violently forwards and sideways as the boat lurched. Because his foot was trapped in the strap, it could not follow the lurch, so it snapped. This is the same syndrome as the snow skier who suffers leg and ankle damage because his safety bindings jam and do not release his twisting boot from the ski.

Head follows tail

These taller seats have also influenced the shape of the console forward of the seat. Obviously they have also become taller. The standing up posture adopted by drivers in waves and in close manoeuvring has led some designers to set the steering wheel flat – a bit like a lorry steering wheel as compared with that of a saloon car. There is some sense in this because it is then easier to turn by the standing helmsman and offers him a more secure handhold. RIB wheels need to be toughies.

The shape of the front end of the seating module has probably been more influenced by the electronics explosion than by any other factor. Our own current boat's 'dashboard' supports hydraulic steering and engine control box, plus a tachometer, a trim and tilt meter and a panel of warning lights for the engine alarms. It also has a magnetic compass, a fluxgate compass, a GPS navigator, a video echo sounder and the VHF radio.

RIB builders now give plenty of thought to the electronics and how to accommodate them. There are some very good consoles on offer and good services for factory fitting a total electronics package. The one problem about them is that their increased width hampers access to the area in front of them. This is, however, only a small problem because the very sharp end of a RIB is a relatively useless and unused part of the boat – rarely visited except when you have plenty of time anyway. Even then, the nimble get there by walking along the tubes.

Interior storage

The logical use for the space immediately under the jockey seat is as the housing for an in-built petrol tank. Its advantages over a couple of standard tanks banging about and vulnerable in the boat are self evident. This siting also puts the fuel reservoir where it is accessible for filling, servicing and repair and where the effects of a drop in level, or the liquid sloshing around, do not upset the boat's trim or any other aspect of its performance.

The forward part of the console beneath the wheel is a wasted area on most boats, yet it can be put to good use. It is not a good place for a big lead acid battery, because it suffers too much rise and fall in waves, but it can be fitted with a shelf to take the VHF and used to house life-jackets, spare ropes and other impedimenta.

This is not a service you would expect a boat builder to offer at low cost, but is eminently the sort of project which a DIY executor could do with a drill and a jigsaw.

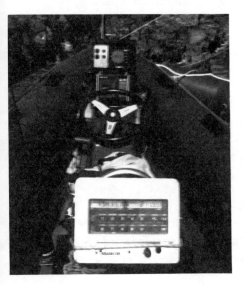

A well-designed instrument console becomes ever more necessary

Good storage and access – but not for all batteries

The sharp end

Only rarely do I need to get right up into the bows of our own boat. It is certainly not the sort of place where you invite anybody to ride, unless they are in the mood for some switchback excitement. It is, however, essential that you are able to get to the nose of the boat in order to tie off the anchor. You only really need enough room to accommodate your legs whilst you reach over to the bow eye, which is just as well because the shape and size of the inflated tubes makes bow room very tight.

Stowing the RIB's anchor and warp will always be a bit of a problem and there have been a number of attempted solutions, none of which has been totally perfect.

An anchor box built as a step on top of the existing floor is one possible way of doing this, but is complicated by the need for drainage. As long as it is kept totally above floor level, two rear holes to let the water brought in by the rope drain into the boat will suffice. If you go below floor level, you need a couple of tubes running back to a well, but even then will need to keep them very clear of weed. The alternative is to sponge out the space after every use.

There are some dangers to making an anchor stowage beneath the deck. There have certainly been two recorded instances of accidents caused by this. Both concerned a RIB in which an anchor space had been created by cutting an oblong in the floor just forward of the console. The space created was given walls of thin plywood and a smear of glass resin.

Typically, one of these was a 5.5 metre craft driven by a 140 hp engine, which the boat builder had declared to be within the hull's tolerance. In our own opinion, such an engine is too heavy and over- powered for this length of boat. This seems to be borne out by the fact that when the boat was accelerated hard into a couple of waves, it folded up across the line of the anchor space.

This incident is related to warn of the consequences of DIY meddling in major modifications to hulls. The floor is often an essential part of their integral strength , rigidity and buoyancy. The hard part of the boat is its most valuable, so you tinker with it at your peril.

Our own anchor is a fairly hefty model on about 6 metres of chain and some 60 metres of medium quality 12 mm rope bought at a boat jumble. The anchor itself is lashed down in the bow, whilst the rope and chain are fed into a box built to the same height and width as the front end of the console.

This box was very simple to make. We merely glued and screwed sections of 10 mm plywood onto some lengths of 25 mm square batten to create the body. The bottom was similarly attached and the lid held in place by Velcro. This means that it can be completely removed for feeding the warp back in. The inside seams and the entire outside of the ensemble was brushed over with orange resin.

The project only took a couple of hours to complete but gives the boat valuable extra stowage space. If the rope is properly fed into the box (never coiled) so that it will just run freely out again, there is still room to put life-jackets, anoraks, a tool kit and vacuum flasks safely in on top of it.

The after box

To make up for the paucity of dry stowage on board, RIB owners get to be very inventive. Our own boat solution has been to fit a very solid wooden box, securely bolted onto the back of the double seat console. This unit has a number of uses.

Its prime function is to take a second 12 v battery in its sealed bottom compartment. The battery is clamped down by metal brackets and connected via a split relay charger. This device allows the engine starting battery to get to full capacity before passing current to the wing battery. It is a standard device, quite common in caravans. We also added a manual switch to isolate this second battery because it feeds all the delicate electronics, which do not react well to the voltage 'spikes' created by engine starting.

Some instruments can be mounted on the external surface of the after chest. Ours has carried a Decca and the engine's oil injection and overheat warnings. The remainder is divided into two shelf compartments. The wide central slot takes the big waterproof box of flares and spares, with the VHF radio as its upstairs neighbour. A perspex cover protects the rig, whose audio is broadcast via a waterproof external speaker. Whoever is riding shotgun becomes the radio operator, whilst the driver just drives.

In harbour, this box is a good extra seat, picnic table and a flat area for simple navigation. Its one down factor is that it takes away a bit of after deck space, but there is still room to stretch out, if you wish to camp on board. We have moulded a quartet of D rings into the floor of the boat to strap down things like picnic baskets, tents, dive cylinders and the portable icebox.

If that list sounds wide, it tells you much about the customised rigid hull inflatable. You fit out the interior to suit your own seagoing lifestyle, which can be anything from Mediterranean lounging, via coastal cruising to diving under the Arctic ice.

Chapter Seven

Adding the Equipment

Those Atlantic College students who pioneered the early RIBs could have had no idea of neither the rapidity nor the magnitude of the type's development. The first boats were comparatively crude, but the craft used by dive clubs, US Coastguard, police, fishery patrols and off-shore rescue services have become miracles of technical and electronic sophistication. There is probably not an instrument nor a marine system in existence that somebody somewhere has not successfully worked on a RIB.

It also comes as a surprise to new owners that the outboard motor will generally cost as much as the boat itself and that the equipment many of us carry costs as much again. In essence, the RIB is no different from any other boat in that it has four levels of gear to be added to the basic hull plus engine combination.

The levels are:
(a) essential sea going equipment
(b) advisable gear
(c) desirable extras
(d) special applications kit

Unfortunately, all this costs money and some of it demands very big money, so a newcomer to RIB ownership really needs a shopping plan – possibly spread over a couple of years. It also has to be realised that how this equipment is stowed and installed can either turn a good boat into a mess, or raise it to the level of a proper little ship.

Steering

For any outboard motor above 50 hp, some form of wheel steering is almost essential. Steering a big boat and power unit by its tiller handle is at best very tiring and at worst not very efficient. This, not only from the point of view of anatomical mechanics, but also in trimming the boat with just a couple of people aboard and allowing the helmsman unobstructed visibility, both before the boat is properly on the plane and when there are several passengers sitting on the sponsons.

Only a few builders who specialise in packages include a steering wheel and a control system in their basic price. Then it will almost inevitably be a totally mechanical system, comprising a worm drive housed in a circular box beneath the wheel, creating its turn on the engine by lengthening and shortening the length of the cable between the wheel and the engine. To accomplish this, the cable (almost as stiff as a rod) needs to be quite thick and to be firmly held onto its supports. It also needs to be laid in straight lines and gentle curves.

There are millions of such steering outfits in regular use. The system works very well and even a hard used, heavy duty rig will last ten years before the parts wear and allow too much play when traversing from one lock to the other. That means that you can go through a quarter of a turn of the wheel before the engine begins to swing.

The major difficulty with cable steering occurs in the close season's idleness. We have had a couple jam up on us because water has seeped into the end fitting at the engine connection. It is virtually impossible to go a whole RIB driving season without getting some sea water over the transom as you go astern, or as the 'pooping wave' overtakes a stopping boat. Inside the cable, the salt and water corrode the unit into immobility.

As ever, prevention is better than cure. If the rear of the boat is always washed in fresh water every time she comes ashore, the problem will generally be avoided. It needs plenty of water with a bit of pressure and then a generous dose of WD40, or similar aqua dispersant cum light lubricant. Do not be apprehensive about spraying the engine: the moderns are pretty tough. A periodic light greasing, or oiling at both ends of the steering cable also helps. If it is really dirty and corroded, about the only way to free it, brute force apart, is to hang the cable up with a drip feed of oil – looking a bit like a hospital saline drip.

A better solution is to fit hydraulic steering, which is now down to RIB parameters in both size and price. It comprises a simple pump in the boss below the steering wheel, feeding a push-pull trombone device through the outboard motor's ride guide mechanism, via a pair of thin, armoured tubes. The drive fluid is ordinary automatic transmission fluid.

The hydraulic ensemble is quite light and very simple to fit. It needs the addition of a drop of fluid at the beginning of each season, but apart from this, it is a good tempered, self lubricating device which largely looks after itself. The hydraulics give an excellent, no play response to the wheel and offer very considerable mechanical advantage when compared to cable steering.

Using it, especially with a large engine, is just like stepping up to a car with power assisted steering. The acid test is that one of our own hydraulic steering systems on a 5.8 metre RIB has withstood five years of about a hundred launches and trips per annum in Summer, alternating with six months idleness each Winter and it is still functioning perfectly.

The anchor

If an anchor and a suitable warp is not the first item on your list of essential equipment, then the list is wrong. The seaman's motto must always be that when something goes radically wrong, you put out the hook so that you stay in a safe place, ie you do not compound the problem by drifting into tide or rocks, or get blown so far out to sea that the warp will no longer reach the bottom.

Rescue service opinionative statistics are that anchoring too late after mechanical breakdown is a major cause of turning an inconvenience into a mishap. This can be especially relevant to the RIB, whose high windage and light construction lend themselves to rapid, wind-borne movement.

This also tells you that the RIB needs an anchor with plenty of holding power and puts you into the never ending debate about which type of anchor is best. The truth is that most of the common varieties are quite good in certain sorts of ground. So we have a problem of choice and a conundrum of how to stow the ironmongery. Over the years we have tried most and a summary of our experience would be as follows.

The folding anchor

The folding anchor was the simplest to carry, but had an annoying habit of folding itself up when it was actually in use on the seabed. In rough conditions of snatch and drag, when you demand most of your anchor anyway, it was difficult to get the locking collar to stay in situ. We had big problems on mixed ground with this one, but should have taken note of the maxim that at sea, things which are designed to fold and collapse, generally do.

The Bruce

The Bruce is a very good anchor with excellent straight line and angular grip when the boat sheers about at the end of its scope. We found that ours was inclined to roll and trip when a changing tide put the anchored boat on a reciprocal, but that it soon dug in again. As an all round performer the Bruce has much in its favour.

On the contra side, especially with reference to RIB usage, it is a very difficult anchor to stow. It needs a lot of space volume and its edges are not very kind to floors, tubes and shins.

The CQR

The CQR has much the same vices and virtues as the Bruce and has the reputation of being an excellent general purpose anchor in a wide variety of holding grounds. It trips less easily as the boat swings and its hinged shank sometimes simplifies getting the anchor clear of ledges.

The CQR will be heavier than an equivalent Bruce, but will be marginally easier to snug down right up in the bow of the boat. Both these anchors will perform better if they are on about twenty feet of solid chain and a nylon, or other 'springy' rope.

The Danforth

The Danforth is a very good anchor in sand and mud. It is one of our own favourites for RIB work, because we only ever need a temporary anchorage – picnic, fishing, diving – and the Danforth is perfectly adequate for such functions. It has the advantage of being light in weight and the flattest and easiest of the three to stow.

The Fortress

The American Fortress anchor is similar to the Danforth in appearance and has three advantages. Firstly, the angle of its flukes can be adjusted to suit the bottom and the angle of pull created by water depth and length of warp. Second, it can be completely dismantled for stowage, but is quick and easy to assemble again. Lastly, it is better used without chain. It needs its shaft kept up to get the best angle, so you save on both weight and capital outlay.

Anchors are always one of the difficult purchase topics of RIB ownership. You pay your money and you make a compromise of your pick.

Life-jackets

A device to keep you afloat if you go over the side should be high on every owner's shopping list. The actual model which you choose rather depends on your sport. Skiers already have buoyancy aids and divers can use a collar ABLJ. For the ordinary boater, the jacket to choose will be governed by who you are, where you go and how confident you are in the water.

The most usual solution is to opt for a collar style lifejacket, which can be filled through its mouth pipe, or activated by compressed gas cylinder. This style is small enough and light enough to encourage you to wear it often, because it does not inhibit your movement around the boat. Putting in a small quantity of air every time you put it on not only increases its safety factors, but also seems to make it sit more comfortably around the neck.

Stowing life-jackets is always a problem. Our present solution is to put them in our bow box. Before this, we kept them in their own canvas bag, which always went home with us for security from thieves – alas, almost always other boat owners.

Paddles

Paddles are probably an essential. It seems a good idea to be able to move the boat over a short distance if the engine fails, even though you will not move it very far, or very fast. Suffice it to say that I am glad that I have them aboard, but my own paddles have rested on top of the internal fuel tank for ten years and have only seen the light of day to be given an occasional lick of varnish.

The Inflator

The inflator should be part of the standard kit and always go to sea with you. The bigger the bellows the better the pump because RIB tubes are much more dependent on the volume of its air than on its pressure. Our flirtation with an electric pump was not a success. It was very heavy on the battery and not really any faster than a crew member exercising some fancy leg and footwork. It was an unnecessary expense, especially as our tubes have never needed anything other than an occasional top up, which can be best affected by a good, traditional style foot inflator. But have one made for the job – not a car tyre pump.

The ropes

The ropes are a boat's badge. "A ship is as good as her warps". You need a minimum of bow, stern and anchor lines. The shore lines should be of good quality nylon, or similar and properly spliced. Poly-propylene is not good, because it floats, which is bad for anchoring.

We get much use out of what we call our Lazy Lines, which are a couple of lengths of good rope with an eye at one end and a medium sized stainless steel snap shackle at the other. To moor the boat, the line can be shackled back to itself, or just clipped onto your own grab line, or another boat's safety rails. If you are diving, you can drop the shackled end over the side ready to hang your weight belt, or goody bag on it when you surface.

We also carry a towing bridle made of thick, spliced and whipped rope, just long enough to snap shackle onto the ski eyes without risk of fouling the propeller. This arrangement centralises the tow rope and spreads the load between two points and also keeps the tug line clear of propeller when you slow down, or a following wave takes the strain off.

The final cordage locker item is the longest length of strong rope you can acquire. Even with a four wheel drive vehicle, you are sure to have a situation where you cannot get your tow hitch close to the boat and have a trailer wheel stuck in soft sand, or a pot-hole

Pandora's Box of flares and spares

caused by a moorings. You might need at least thirty metres to reach terra firma for the tow truck on occasions.

The spares and flares box

The spares and flares box is one to build up over a period of time, Christmases and birthdays. It should be a real treasure trove of bits and pieces, some of which will find regular use and others which you hope never to use at all. By far the best method of carrying this very valuable piece of cargo in the RIB, is to protect it in the sort of screw top, waterproof container used for off-shore flare packs.

The more you fill the box to stop the items bouncing around, the safer they will be. Until your collection builds up, wrap everything in cloth and fill the gaps with squares of material which can be used as dusters and cleaning rags. You then have a very useful piece of gear, which can be lashed safely in the boat, but also taken home away from the eyes and hands of the crooked.

In a moment of total crisis, the box could be thrown overboard and would not only float, but would also give some temporary buoyancy to a weak swimmer. Typically amongst its contents will be:-

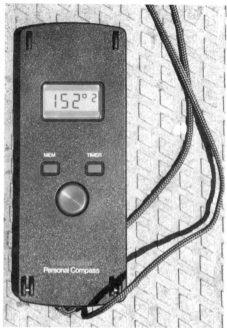

Make the hand bearing compass also usable as a steering tool

An electronic handbearing compass is useful – but its operation is a skill to be learned

Hand bearing-compass

A hand bearing-compass, must be of the sort that not only allows you to take bearings for navigation, or if you are involved in a search and rescue incident, but also has the sort of dual purpose graphics making it suitable for emergency steering.

The graphics notation need not be in single degrees. In fact spaces of 2° or even 5° are plenty good enough for the envisaged applications and are much simpler to operate. This rules out some of the types of electronic compass, which anyway do not take kindly to a permanently damp environment and also lose their accuracy when tilted.

Some of the hand bearing compasses made of ABS or other plastic are ideal for RIBs. They are small, tough, simple to read and have a flat, friction promoting format, which means that they stay where they are put when places on seats and consoles. They also hang lightly and comfortably around your neck and inside your oilskin.

Flares

Flares are a topic of never ending debate. The RIB owner working to a budget needs to let practical and economic sense apply according to how, where and when he uses his boat. He must make judgements and balance the probabilities.

The principles of pyrotechnic generated requests for immediate assistance remain that a very bright red light is set to burn at altitude to catch the casual observer's eye. It should be followed by something which burns for long enough to let the competent get a bearing on you, or at least to note your direction. This is most usually red, or orange smoke, which has the secondary function of showing possible rescuers and helicopters the line of wind and drift.

The useful revolver flare

Those are the principles which guide what you buy and they are modified by where you take your boat. A RIB making regular solo channel crossings, or going to fish and dive off-shore wrecks, should have at least two "coastal" size, red parachute flares and a medium size smoke cartridge.

Inshore, you keep the smoker, but could be served by one of the excellent new breed of mini flares housed in a revolving magazine like a Colt hand-gun. This device is totally waterproof and can even by taken sub aqua. It is very safe, because it cannot be fired horizontally, but it can also be operated with one hand.

The flares themselves have very adequate burn and luminosity levels for their rated distance. When I launched a red to summon assistance to a yacht that I was unable to reach because by own boat was dried out at her moorings, it set the 999 calls ringing from a wide geography of shore viewers. I could have fired a salvo to compensate for the short burn.

The flares can also be purchased in white for warning off and green for attracting attention. The device is small, tough, safe, practical and a valuable addition to the box.

Signalling devices

Safety signalling devices like a whistle, a waterproof torch and a mirror make good Christmas gifts, their use expectancy is low in an era where 90% of rescue assistance is summoned by VHF radio, but they are, nonetheless worth having and will generally find a secondary function.

Engine spares

Engine spares are an absolute ingredient of the crash box recipe. They should include a starting cord (any thin rope will do), fuses, spark plugs and some WD40 or similar. Many outboard motor problems are related to the fuel supply and especially to the ingress of air. A spare fuel pressure bulb, an engine case attachment and a couple of jubilee clips will always bring peace of mind. We assume that you have tne tools to fit these things and also to remove the propeller. If you carry a spare prop, you should also include any thrust washers used by your make of engine, plus a castle nut and a couple of split pins.

Odds and ends

These could include some insulating tape, a small tube of silicone, some instant adhesive, a small reel of cod line or whipping twine, a few stainless steel self tapping screws and some nuts, washers and bolts. A couple of bungy cords are useful from time to time and a ship without a good knife and a practical first aid kit is not a ship at all. Also ensure that you have a spare ignition key and kill switch, not only on the curly lanyard, but also with a cord which is used to tie the ensemble to a steering cable, or a part of the console, so that if it is yanked out in a hurry, it does not go over the side

Binoculars

Binoculars and boats seem to be inseparable. For RIB owners, the mistake is to be tempted either for high magnification, or to go for cheapness. The former means that you cannot focus properly because of boat movement and the latter generally has an objective lens of such poor light gathering and such narrow diameter (giving a small field of view) that you cannot retain the target inside its circumference.

The best RIB binoculars are the medium size, fixed focus or zoom, rubber armoured variety of 6-8 times magnification and adequate diameter front lens. You should remove them from the boat and give them a wash after every trip, otherwise they will soon develop cloudy lenses and the white powdery garnish denoting the first signs of salt air corrosion. Some of armoured miniature binoculars are also well worth considering.

Compass

The RIB compass is not a problem in itself. Difficulties occur when other instruments like a tachometer or a VHF radio speaker are placed close enough to affect the accuracy and North seeking alignment of the magnetics. Actually choosing the compass is only complicated by the wide choice from excellently engineered models. The usual style is the largest glass dome which the console will take, with the instrument's main body dropped below its surface. The compass should be picked for a very clear display, but do not be tempted into paying extra for single 360° notation, you will not be able to use such precision anyway.

A person that tells you that he can keep a RIB within 5° of the rhumb line heading using a conventional card compass at sea, undoubtedly spends more time at the bar than at the helm. There are a number of reasons for this, even when one discounts the RIB's exciting liveliness. Very few small boat compasses are accurate to anything less than two to five degrees. Most boats have inherent magnetic anomalies which reduce card accuracy and a number do not even have the lubber line set absolutely fore and aft. There are also drivers who do not sit square, so are not really steering where they think.

However, the main reason why driving the RIB on a card compass can only ever be an approximation is because the accepted industry time for such a compass to resettle after a 360° rotation is – very surprisingly – in excess of fifty seconds. On a lively boat, the card is very rarely steady within a 5° vector, but this is good enough for inshore work, where the distances are short enough to cope with the error and where there will probably be plenty of correcting landmarks.

The fluxgate compass is no longer a mystery

Electronic compass

The electronic compass is the serious RIB driver's way of solving all
the problems of mounting the unit for accuracy and of coping with
a bucking, gyrating card. It is sometimes called a fluxgate compass,
because the heading sensor is a coil, flux or toroid, either
suspended on a plumb bob, or mounted on a pivot.

When this wire element is excited by a small electric current, it
returns a voltage which varies in direct proportion to the flux's
alignment with the Earth's lines of magnetic force. Put very briefly,
this voltage is always at its maximum when the alignment is North-
South and at its minimum on the East-West axis. In between, the
returned signal is directly proportional, which means –
simplistically – that the element always knows where it is in
relation to North because of the level of induced voltage.

Fluxgate compass engineers have devised a number of ways of solving how to cope with the fact that two maxima and minima voltages will occur in a 360° rotation and have come up with a compass which is an ideal RIB tool for a number of reasons.

A) Because the system is electronically driven, the resettling time, even after the most violent changes of course, can be counted in small fractions of a second. In normal, navigational use, there is practically no swing. The boat's head is where the compass says it is aligned.

B) Because the display of a good fluxgate compass is separate from the main part of the system, the actual heading sensor can be mounted in the dry and close to the epicentre of the boat's pitch and roll, where it is protected from the elements and subject to minimum movement.

Our own is low down in the centre of the console and is connected by waterproof plugs to a display unit mounted in a pod, which can be removed from the console top after every trip.

C) This sort of compass is easy to use because the display can be configured in an analogue pointer, or 360° digital notation, or both. The rapid settlement time makes for very precise, reliable course keeping, which is further enhanced by some of the electronically enabled functions.

All our long passages are made entirely with the compass in 'Off Course' mode, which is engaged as soon as the boat is settled on its heading. This lights up a single LCD vertical spike at the twelve o'clock position. Thereafter, if the boat's head drops off one degree to port, a second spike appears at the left of the first. A five degree error, illuminates spikes from eleven o'clock to midnight and so on. By keeping the screen clear of LCD spikes, you know that he boat is right on its intended heading.

D) The fluxgate compass usually incorporates an automatic correction of deviation package. When the boat is driven through 360° at sea, the elements sense any internal magnetic aberrations on different headings and the software applies the corrections necessary to cancel out all fore and aft and thwartship anomalies. If you add some new equipment, you swing the compass and it corrects itself into accuracy again.

The disadvantage of the sort of compass described above is that it is very expensive. If you are racing, or covering distances up to twenty miles off-shore, the money is well spent. There is little point in having a satellite navigator to indicate a line to a wreck, or a landfall, if the compass cannot match its performance. (Using the Cross Track Error function of a Decca or GPS is not a feasible way of driving a fast boat.)

There is a new breed of smaller integral electronic compasses with the flux element contained in the same unit as the display. These are a satisfactory compromise for inshore work, but suffer the disadvantage of a sensor mounted in a less stable location and exposed to water and weather. Their stability suffers from pitch and roll effects because an electronic compass must have its flux element parallel to the flat plane of the floor to be accurate.

This effect is easy to demonstrate. The electronic hand bearing compass on the desk as I write is aligned 247° in the flat position. Tilting it about 25° towards me changes this figure to 232° and 226° appears in the display when I raise the front end as though the boat was going over a wave.

Such a unit is very practical as long as the navigator is aware of the effects. Much the same happens when our own compass (costing several hundred pounds) is subjected to the effects of the RIB's powerful acceleration. The plumb bob is pulled away from the vertical by the G forces and the flux element comes out of parallel alignment. For a few seconds, the digital display goes haywire, but rapidly settles again when the boat's nose drops and she is running flat on the plane.

Electronics

Boat electronics are at a very sophisticated level, largely because the sub aqua fraternity has espoused the RIB as the ideal dive vehicle and have clamoured for instruments to suit. (The angling and racing people have also clamoured.) So, we have a superb range of position fixing systems and video echo sounders all making RIB cruising, diving, fishing and pottering generally much more efficient and generally a lot more fun.

Decca – GPS – or Loran-C?

The choice of a position fixing and general navigation system is really developing into something of a non contest for RIB owners. To understand the rules, you need to know a bit about the systems.

Decca and Loran-C are both radio based systems depending on the reception of radio waves coming from several directions at once. The transmitting stations are called Master and Slaves and their outputed waves travel omni directionally. The best way to visualise the signal pattern is to see it as three pebbles dropped into various places of a pond at the same time. The ripples travel out in concentric circles and every place where two (or three) of them coincide makes a position fix.

Loran has the greater range of the two, but Decca is usually the more accurate in most European waters, where both are operational in different areas. Unfortunately, both suffer the vagaries of radio propagation conditions, which makes the quality of the signals – and hence the position fix – drop off at night. The signals are also affected by Winter weather and rain storms.

The satellite derived Global Positioning System suffers none of these minus qualities. The twenty plus US military satellites are in very carefully checked and controlled orbits and work by the measurement of time. Briefly, the on-boat computer knows at exactly which micro second the signal was released and is similarly precise about reception. By measuring the time taken by these signals to reach the antenna, it can measure how far each satellite was from the boat at the time and from this data compute the navigator's classic cocked hat.

That is a simplistic explanation of a superlative system, with an accuracy precise to fifteen metres but, for civilian purposes, deliberately diluted to one hundred metres.

All three navigation methods have apparatus suitable for RIB life. There is also an emerging range of dual instruments which compute position and speed, whilst also simultaneously giving a video picture of the seabed. This equipment is small, tough and environment proof.

Combined position fixer and echo sounder is the perfect RIB navigator

We could discuss boat electronics for many more paragraphs, but here it is enough to point out that they exist in RIB style and are beginning to appear at sensible prices. None of my own boats has had an A frame for lights, for the very simple reason that we do not take them out at night and prefer to have radio and GPS antennae mounted on their own masts, which are not above the outboard and, therefore, less affected by its spurious electrical noises.

There are a number of RIBs around with more aerials and as much electronic equipment as the average warship. And why not? If you have the sort of boat which will go anywhere and do anything asked of it, there is a lot of fun in making it as sophisticated as the pennies will allow.

That is fun. In all the writer's pontificating about safety and good seamanship, we sometimes lose sight of the fact that for most seagoers, the main reason for being out there is to have fun.

Flight deck. Note the rigid bow section

Chapter Eight

The Engine

The RIB and its engine must be seen together. Even without going to the ridiculous scenario of trying to fit a 40 hp outboard onto a 3.5 metre boat, it is logical to assume that not all engines are suitable for all RIBs and neither are they all suitable for all applications. A water-skier needing a powerful, fast accelerating tug to get him out of 'the hole', requires a different power unit from the commercial fisherman, whose engine might be running continuously for 12 hours a day on six days a week.

In the early RIB days, choice of engine was decided by Mr Hobson, who decreed that it should be an outboard motor or nothing. Nowadays, however, you could be offered a choice of diesel inboard, sterndrive, jet drive, diesel outboard, four stroke outboard, twin two stroke, or single two stroke outboards and a bewildering array of propellers.

The problem of the big inboard is, yes, its high capital cost, but also its weight. It confines RIB usage to places where a big, heavy boat can be safely manoeuvred on its trailer over ground where its wheels are not likely to sink into soft mud. Diesel inboards are for big, off-shore hulls where good acceleration and high speed are not essential factors and where the running periods are long enough for the engine to get thoroughly warm. Diesels thrive on continuous work.

The diesel outboard is coming down in size and weight, but still has many of the disadvantages inherent in its inboard cousin. It is still a heavy and expensive lump to hang onto the transom, but has found some favour with commercial fish farmers, who are increasingly turning to the sea-kindliness and versatility of the RIB as a prime work boat.

Outdrives and jet drives have their virtues, but their vices will always be a greater deterrent to installation by RIB owners, who are more likely to be leisure users than professional operators. Most of us pleasure seekers are looking for manageable capital outlay, a load which can be towed by the family car and launched over a beach by a couple of people, even in shallow water. nonetheless, we also wish to have a water vehicle which is exciting to drive and to ride. This means that the petrol fuelled, two stroke outboard, with its low weight, high speed and good acceleration is by far the most agreeable RIB partner.

Having seen this particular light, the choice then becomes one of a single engine or twins. It is here that writers step into the minefield, because the protagonists of one or the other tend to be like fervent politicians and religious maniacs of all faiths. They have beliefs which are very difficult to modify. All we can do is to set out the facts.

These become more important if you are buying used or reconditioned outboard motors separate from the boat. This is a grey area in which it is very simple to end up with an unsuitable engine, or lose a lot of money, or both. The case of a friend who bought an ex military outboard which had been reconditioned by an expert is not uncommon. The engine ran perfectly, but just did not seem to have the punch required to drive the boat. A long and frustrating analysis showed that the motor had been modified to take a low compression cylinder head.

We also have details of a diver who purchased a pair of 50 hp engines only to find that they were short shaft models requiring a 15" transom, but his boat need a 20" drop to get the props down where they would bite. He had the choice of retro-fitting two expensive engine shaft extensions rods, or of cutting a 5" oblong out of the transom. The poor man opted for this second solution, but the boat never seemed to balance properly thereafter and was very vulnerable to swamping when put astern.

The moral to these case histories is that matching engine to RIB is not only essential and expensive, but needs to begin with the basic research of both boat and engine brochures. Firstly you ask about the transom depth of the boat. There is not much loss if this has to be trimmed by an inch or so. Then you scan the engine brochures. Some manufacturers quote a "recommended transom height" for their outboards – probably fifteen or twenty inches. Others will say something like "60 hp shaft length: short 390 mm, long 515 mm. A third maker could replace short with "Standard" and even offer an "Ultra long" option.

Similarly, some installers prefer to keep the shaft a bit longer, then to put a small batten beneath the engine mounting bracket in order to get the propeller up where it will give the best top speed for skiing and racing, without constantly trimming the engine out on the hydraulics.

So, even at this very fundamental level, there are plenty of options and, by implication, plenty of scope for being too hasty and possibly getting it wrong. The RIB is much too much of a thoroughbred for such abuse. Properly set up, with entirely appropriate engine, or engines, it will match most hulls for pace and will better them all for versatility and sea keeping.

One engine or two

Before resolving the one engine or two conundrum, we need to ask ourselves why we are thinking about two engines anyway. Here it has to be admitted that very many RIB owners are admirers of the RNLI and very influenced by lifeboat practices. The Atlantic 21 is fitted with twin engines because it is asked to operate in places and conditions where a swamping, or a fouled and damaged propeller is a real possibility.

Thus, the conclusion must be that the second engine has only one purpose, which is to enhance safety and to cover its fellow in case of breakdown. This short conclusion is not to decry, or to diminish the search for greater safety and independence, but one should also ask if there might be cheaper and more convenient ways of

The attraction of twin engines

achieving the same ends, especially in a boat which does not go very far off-shore, or in one which is not used in severe weather, nor at times where there are no other vessels out and about.

Bearing in mind the very high quality and very low breakdown incidence of a well maintained present generation outboard motor, the RIB owner might be just as well served by a powerful single unit and – say – a 5 hp long shaft donkey engine with a remote tank, which could also be used as a reserve to the main. Such an engine would push a 5.5 metre RIB along at an approximate 4 knots get-you-home speed. The reduction in weight and savings in other areas make this an interesting proposition and gives an engine combination suitable for a family runabout.

If twin engines are fitted they should ideally be on totally separate, but switchable fuel and electrical supplies. When outboards refuse to function, the most common reasons are electrical problems and starting, or fuel which is either contaminated, or leaking air into the system. Twin engines connote the extra expense and the added weight of two batteries and two adequately sized fuel tanks.

The economics and tolerances must also be weighed up in other respects. Twin 50 hp engines do not equate to the same thrust as a single 100 hp unit. In power and speed terms, twin fifties are the equivalent of about 85 horsepower, even before allowing the extra weight. On something like a 5.75 m – 6.0 m RIB a single 90 hp engine should give a cruising speed of about 25 knots at 4000 RPM and four gallons an hour. The 50s will need to work at higher revs to attain the same speed and will burn at least two gallons per hour more.

If we lay out a comparative table for twins versus singles it would currently be:-

	TWIN 50s	SINGLE 90
Capital cost	£6590	£5530
Petrol + oil per hour	6 x £2 = £12	4 x £2 = £8
Service charges	£100	£50
Weight	86.5 x 2 = 173 kg	120 kg

To these contra factors must be added the cost of the power to weight effect on the tow car and the extra costs of installation, which needs double steering rods and twin looms.

Many newcomers also expect the double rig to handle like a twin screw ship. In practice, the RIB's twin props are not contra rotating and are so close together that there is not an enormous, controlled turning moment created by putting one engine ahead and the other astern. Most of us who own twin screw RIBs rarely use them in this mode.

At rest, a twin engined boat will always look down by the stern and this extra weight is also drag when you are getting up onto the plane. You must also accept that when the two throttle levers are

Twin motors inevitably make her look down by the stern

pushed forward together, the fact that they are aligned with each other does not necessarily mean that the engine revs are the same. Cables stretch, levers get sluggish etc. The twin driver is constantly adjusting one lever or the other to stop the boat pulling one way, unless he happens to be a very competent engine tuner.

Conclusions

Let me now put all my cards on the table and say that I have owned RIBs with both single and dual engine configurations. In making long, off-shore passages, there is great peace of mind to be derived from twin engines, although our one failure was when our buddy boat caught a rope, which wrecked both his props, so we towed him home to get it sorted out. Off-shore, even with twin engines a partner boat and a donkey engine would be ideal.

Thus, if you are planning to spend a lot of time off-shore, or plan to make unaccompanied cross Channel voyages, then you will feel safer with twin engines

Closer to the shore, most of us can feel quite secure and enjoy the diminished costs and loads of a faster single unit.

Having said these things and having really enjoyed all my boats, we should never forget that, for most of us, owning and using a boat is pleasure. If part of that pleasure is the pride and the satisfied security of owning the engine format which gives you most personal satisfaction and fun, the choice and the privilege is entirely yours. That is the beauty of RIBbing. It can be all things to all owners.

The starting system

Whether your outboard is started by electrics or by the old fashioned 'Armstrong' method of a pull cord, will be decided by the manufacturer's rating system. There are very few manual start (or manually steered) outboards above 50 horsepower, but I should never contemplate the purchase of any engine which did not have the facility for rope starting.

This is not only an emergency function, but can also make life much easier when you have the spark plugs out and wish to turn the engine over for such routine maintenance as getting some more engine seal lubricant into the chamber during the Winter lay-up.

Electrics make RIB sense, especially now that most of us fit a range of electronics, but we must also consider the supply. Look at the brochures. If you can run to an engine which has an electricity system which is both rectified and regulated, the kinder it will be to your instruments. Their safety and performance can also be affected by your choice of battery.

The sort of completely sealed, spillproof, zero maintenance battery which is quite common in the automotive trade has not had the best press in some sections of the big boat press. Because of the RIB's rough life and lively nature, such batteries have great appeal in spite of this. One can only speak as one finds. Our current boat has had two, small, no maintenance batteries installed in adequately ventilated locations for the past four years. During that time we have done nothing other than re-grease and tighten the connectors from time to time. The batteries have never been put on an external charger, but have always retained sufficient voltage to restart our 3 cylinder, 90 hp engine, after long periods of inactivity including the six month Winter lay-up time.

The fuel system

How a two stroke outboard motor is fuelled cannot really be divorced from how it is lubricated. The trend is generally away from the pre- mixing of petrol and oil towards oil injection which, as its name implies, automatically mixes the carburant and lubricant. The theoretical advantage is that the engine is always being given the amount of oil which it needs.

This is to say that at slow speed and low RPM, the demand is small, so precisely satisfying this level of requirement will prevent oiled up spark plugs and sticky valves, because they have been fed too much oil without being hot enough to dispose of it properly. Most of us who mix up 2-stroke fuel are cautiously generous with the amount of oil we put in – and then generally add a little drop for luck. Most pre-mix outboards are over-oiled, which is almost as bad as the converse.

It was also very noticeable that even though we switched up from a 2 cylinder 55 hp pre-mix engine to a 3 cylinder 90 hp oil injection model, which used more fuel for the year, our oil bill was about 50% reduced.

To match lubricant to engine RPM rate is commonly achieved by a small pump driven directly off the crank. The faster the engine goes, the harder the pump works and the more oil is squirted in. There the similarity stops and the differences between the two usual types of mid range and high horsepower outboards become apparent.

Basically they depend on where the actual amalgamation takes

Japanese technology makes some very reliable outboards

place. It can be a a single pipe delivery, injecting and mixing the oil just before it passes into the carburettor. This has, for some time, been the preferred system of American designers. To avoid confusion it should perhaps be called oil mix.

Japanese designers have largely brought their engine lubrication system for outboards across from technology employed on motor cycles. It employs a crank driven pump feeding a separate pipe to each cylinder. There the oil is injected behind the reed valve and is atomised under manifold pressure. The resultant fine cloud of oil is then sprayed over all the engine's internal moving parts just as though an aerosol is being employed.

Both systems are well tried, very refined by experience and very reliable. Oil pump failure is an almost unknown outboard motor malady.

Most outboard motors require the highest octane petrol available and some have the reputation of starting more easily if lead free petrol is avoided. It pays to ask your supplier about this but, as far as we know, all the outboards suitable for RIBs will run on leaded or unleaded fuel.

Features and accessories

The outboard really has come a long league hence from its early days and its unenviable reputation for unreliability, oily plugs, poor starting qualities and high causative consumption of bad language. Our modern high technology machines bristle with safety and back-up features.

Our present engine, for example, boasts high output electronic ignition, but this science is also carried over to other operations. If we let the lube in the oil injection reservoir get too low, a warning buzzer sounds, a light flashes and the engine automatically cuts itself back to very low revs, where it will continue to run quite safely for another couple of hours. You might only travel at mackerel spinning speed, but at least you will get home in time to cook them for tea.

In similar vein, if the cooling water pump impeller jams (unlikely) or a plastic bag gets sucked into the intake, the electronics take over to sound the alarm and to reduce the engine's revs to a level at which it can continue to run without damage. This RPM reduction is also brought into play by the over-rev limiter.

The propeller is occasionally forced into high speed cavitation, which should more properly be called aeration, because the blades are spinning in air, so have no retarding aqua force to control their speed. This happens if you fly the boat off the top of a wave and it drags air down with it when it lands in the trough. It can also occur if the boat is driven into a tight, hard, full lock circle and held there. As the hull heels, the propeller blade tips come out of the water and drag air down automatically.

Electro-hydraulic trim and tilt has many times proved its value. We have explained, elsewhere, how this feature is used to control the boat when it is being driven down waves and its uses in shallow, rocky places are obvious. Because our own crew generally comprises just two of us, one can walk ashore to get the trailer, whilst the other can trim the engine right up on the electrics and drive the boat right onto the trailer in very shallow water. You cannot do this (even with a mob-handed crew) with manual tilt motors. This one feature alone has saved us many muscle straining miles of pulling a heavy, draggy boat over soft sand because it could only be loaded in deep water.

On the trailer, with the engine titled for towing, a touch on the tilt mechanism's down button, electrically forces the engine onto its mechanical road stops and holds it firmly there against the jolting of road bumps.

When you go shopping for an engine to suit your RIB, these are the things which should be in your mind. You should also have a look at what instruments are included as standard. A tachometer is an absolute essential and a trim and tilt meter advisable. In the de-luxe extras class, a fuel flow meter comes high on the list.

Also be aware of the boat builders recommended maximum engine horsepower rating. It is worth remembering that even though more power will always cost more money, all outboards are very thirsty at the top end of their rev range. The fuel consumption graph does not go up in the straight diagonal line of a direct proportion equation, but curves sharply upwards between – say – 4500 RPM and the usual 5500 RPM maximum. A big engine like a 100 hp running at 75% power will be using considerably less fuel than a 60 hp model running at 95% to achieve the same speed.

You might soon recoup the capital outlay, which could give a bit more to spend on some more equipment, or perhaps a better trailer.

Chapter Nine

The RIB Trailer

Your RIB trailer needs a fair amount of planning and consideration for a number of reasons.

1 Many new owners are surprised to learn that the boat trailer alone, can cost as much as 15% of the value of the boat and outboard motor together.

2 There is little virtue in having a very versatile boat, but confining yourself to a marina because your car will not tow the outfit. There also seems less virtue in being forced to change your car because the present one will not cope with the combined weight of the boat, outboard, fuel, equipment and trailer. This has happened. So, in planning your RIB strategy, the trailer and the car must be included as an integral part of the whole project. They are inseparable in practical terms.

3 To get the best use from the RIB, the trailer must be capable of launching it over a wide variety of terrains from steeply sloping slipways to the soft sand of an inner harbour.

4 About 90% of all damage to boats occurs on the land and much of this happens either when the hull is being winched on to the trailer, or when it is on the trailer and either being manoeuvred into a special place, or is being towed at speed.

In summary, your trailer must be legal, light but strong, suitable for your vehicle, safe on the road and easy to manage with the boat on its back, or when being loaded and unloaded.

From our lounge window, we see a hundred and more boats a year launched on a variety of trailers. Almost without exception, the ones with the problems have been those who have tried to build a trailer on the cheap and have either skimped on materials, or been woefully short on expertise. We have seen them so massive that they sank into the soft sand of the harbour and so weak that their backs have broken on a famous hump on the hill up from the quay. We have also had them jump off the ball hitch and simply corrode to uselessness in a season.

Trailers for our generation of light, high rev cars are a very specialist engineering concept. The only two safe ways for a non engineer to get one which meets all the requirements are to buy a kit of parts from one of the few companies who offer them, or to have a proper, commercially built trailer to fit the RIB of your choice.

The trailered RIB is not a problem

Road Safety

This is not the place to discuss the way in which cars and boat trailers are driven on the road. It is a skill soon learned, especially as the current breed of trailers is so efficient that the driver is in some danger of forgetting that he has one in tow. For us, comment on trailer road safety is more a matter of maintenance and attachment to protect the boat.

Our sphere of interest neatly divides into four separate areas covering wheels and bearings, jockey wheels, ball hitches and how the boat is actually secured on the trailer.

Wheel Bearings

Failed wheel bearings were almost always the cause of the listing boat trailers which you used to see stranded beside major roads and neglect the most common cause of the accident. We all tend to be so proud of the boat that it takes all our time, so we neglect the trailer. If a bearing fails and the loaded trailer slews across the road, the consequences to boat and to third parties are unthinkable.

Boat trailers regularly immersed in salt water and left standing idle for long periods, really do have a very rough life. The precautions are to hose the outfit down with a generous amount of fresh water after every use if possible and to keep the wheel bearings well filled with grease.

Our own experience confirms that using a proprietary, waterproof trailer grease reduces the water getting into the hubs by about fifty percent. How often you service them obviously depends on mileage. The effectiveness of the grease is diminished by getting warm on long journeys and by salt water leaking in. Our own trailer only runs about a mile to the sea, so we find that as long as the bearing cap is lifted off about every twenty launches, or the cavity is filled via a grease nipple, the bearings cope with the immersions. At the beginning of each season and about half way through, we remove the wheel altogether and completely clean off and replace all the existing grease. In this way, we remove so much water, grit and sand that a set of wheel bearings can be made to last for two or three years, even with heavy use.

When the bearings are replaced, one set is always kept as a back-up spare and I would certainly never undertake a long tow without a spare, or without servicing the existing bearings prior to departure.

Jockey wheels

These have always been one of the banes of our boating life. Even with regular washing, they still manage to corrode into immobility. Most of them are made with the caravan and other land based pursuits in mind, so the materials do not take kindly to sea water. The units are put together of metals having such vastly different galvanic properties that they almost seem to eat each other.

After much heart and wallet searching, we look after our jockey wheels as well as we are able, but accept that they probably only have a two year life span used where we habitually launch over sand and through a mixture of soft mud, mooring chains and stone. When we need a replacement, we now ignore boat retailers with the exaggerated prices, but go to camping and caravan centres, or to depots specialising in the supply of parts and spares to commercial operators and those who are building trailers from kits. A saving of about 33% is the norm for our trouble.

Our search is always for a wheel with the widest possible standard jockey wheel tyre we can find. Like the trailer's main wheels, the broader the load bearing base, the better the progress when the going gets soft and the less we are likely to damage the boat. We stick to standard wheels because they are cheaper to replace. Our flirtations with strange, ultra wide jockey wheel contraptions have been expensive and ineffective.

Ball hitch

The ball hitch will not generally give any trouble as long as you take the usual precautions. It needs a regular wash in fresh water and a dab of grease, or a squirt of heavy oil, onto all the moving parts from time to time. It also pays to clean it up with a wire brush and to renew and to increase the grease coating if you are leaving the trailer outside or for the Winter.

Safety strop

A safety strop is a very simple idea, practically standard on caravans, but less often seen on boat trailers. Having seen the results of a trailer which jumped off and ran back down the hill into the harbour car park in my home town, I welcome the piece of mind of having a strong safety rope running from the trailer to a strong attachment point on the vehicle. Its purpose is simply to hold the boat trailer attached until you get the combination under control if you have a fault. At the very least, it would stop the trailer careering across the road into someone else.

Front mounted ball hitch

A front mounted ball hitch has been one of the best couple of pounds which we have ever spent. One of the local pleasures hereabouts is watching the antics of boat owners reversing down the narrow slipway. If you can mount a ball on the front bumper, you just drive down in forward gear. This is safer and certainly much quicker and is especially useful if you are in the Bank Holiday Sunday launching queue.

The convenient front mounted ball hitch

Trailer fixings

Trailer fixings are as variable as trailers. The golden rule, however, is to keep them as simple as possible and this can be very simple if your trailer is properly matched to the boat. By this I mean that when the boat is winched tightly up to the rubber bow snubber and the front end is supported by it, the boat should not wobble.

If the trailer is suitable, the keel of the boat should be firmly on at least three rollers, one of which should be right under the heel of the transom, so that it gives the maximum amount of support to the engine. This is a very vulnerable area of trailer boating in general and of RIB porterage is particular. A heavy outboard tugging and swinging on the leverage of a tall transom can seriously stretch and weaken the areas where the transom is bonded onto the sponsons.

The full keel support can be a DIY project

This is such an important art of boat and trailer life that it demands extra care. In addition to ensuring that the very tip of the keel (minimum overhang) is resting on something solid and that the motor is firmly down on its electro hydraulics, it pays to invest in one of the proprietary hydraulic, or spring loaded devices, which fit between a solid part of the trailer and the leg of the outboard motor, just below the cavitation plate.

As a personal foible, I always back up this longitudinal rigidity with something to inhibit side to side wobble. Here the ski hooks come into their own as attachment points to pull the boat hard down.

These two stern ropes will also make up for any wobbles induced because the side supports to the hull might not be absolutely in line, or because a micro space between support and boat has been caused by a little bit of GRP warping.

Our final trailer lashing is a bowline through the bow eye, with a short rope around the trailer, sweated down as tightly as we can get it. When it is in place, we give a final tweak to the winch handle to ensure that it is tight and that the ratchet brake is in place. Our winch has a strap, which is less prone to stretching (and much less dangerous to crew members) than a wire cable. It creates good friction.

The winch ratchet does not have a locking pin, but we have never found this to be necessary. If the boat is firmly pulled down by the triangle of ropes, the winch takes very little stress, so is not inclined to shake loose. We also feel more at ease by knowing that if the winch did slacken of its own accord, there is no way in which the boat could slide off the trailer even as we climb the very steep hill leading from the harbour to our garage.

People sometimes ask why we do not use a couple of wide ratchet straps over the top of the boat. We confess that we bought them but have discontinued their use. RIBs are a bit different from solid boats. You can put one on the trailer in the heat at the tail end of a warm Summer afternoon and pull the lateral straps down taut. Then the evening cools and the breeze of towing cools the tubes and causes the air inside to contract slightly. Then the sponson goes a little bit 'squidgy', the strops are no longer taut, so they begin to chafe the fabric of the boat.

It makes more sense to ensure that the boat is well propped by the trailer rollers, snubbers and supports and to make all your attachments to the solid hull and transom. Such a system becomes doubly important if you are thinking of buying one of the extra wide boats aimed at the diving market. Some of these are wider than the legal towable limit, so their tubes must be deflated for road work. This means that a boat cover is a waste of money and that lateral, or cross over straps are totally ineffective.

There is a set of laws governing trailers, weights and the relationship between the tow car and its pulled unit. These change so rapidly, especially under the influence of EEC harmonisation, that any analysis would soon be out of date. The official boating organisations always have up-to date information and the trailer manufacturers are also helpful.

To bring our literary wheel full circle again, we must not forget that a boat spends more of its time on land than on the sea, so we must give this aspect of its life a proportionate amount of our attention.

The trailer balance must be correct

Chapter Ten

More About Driving and Using

The RIB is such a super all-rounder and can perform so many tasks, that you are certain to be asked to demonstrate them at some time during your stewardship of such a boat. This is, of course, a compliment to both the boat and the skipper and, provided you are not putting either of them in danger, these extra seamanship tasks are huge fun and very satisfying to complete.

During my own association with outboard driven rigid hulls, the jobs and requests list has been very interesting. We have assisted with a number of Coastguard search and rescue incidents. On one day, the authorities asked us to go ten miles out to sea to free a yacht whose propeller was fouled by a lobster pot line. We have delivered commercial divers and a camera crew out to a cable laying ship. Tornado has several times been 15 miles off-shore to act as guard and spotter boat for the Cowes-Torquay-Cowes power-boat classic and has done the same for inshore races. Running as rescue boat to the local sailing club has always been a welcome and welcomed part of our life in a seaside community. Acting as Gate Boat for the UK Fireball dinghy championships was one of the most demanding of all jobs. Only a good RIB could have done it safely.

Because the tasks which your RIB might be asked to do, you – as skipper – need to learn the boat handling skills to enjoy them. My own earlier background was in fishing and passenger boats, which are very traditional and have a good basis of handed-down expertise. When I became fascinated with RIBs, this early training served me well, but it was not enough. The RIB's handling pluses, minuses and excitements demand a totally different set of seamanship talents, which do not replace the basics, but must be seen as extras to them.

Gate boat for the UK Fireball Championships

Club rescue boat

The first appreciation of this comes when you are invited to act as guard boat to a sailing event. In the old days of doing this with a displacement boat, which more or less stays where it is put, picking up capsized dinghies was so difficult that we mostly did not bother, but towed them in as they were. We were also frequently in the way of competitors because we needed to be in the centre of the course.

The RIB is so quick that it can patrol around the outside of whatever race course pattern is being sailed – triangle, diamond or sausage. If someone is in trouble, you can generally be with them in a few seconds.

The best technique thereafter is to make one pass down the side of the dinghy to ascertain that none of its crew needs immediate assistance. Then run about fifty yards down wind, down waves, or down-tide (whichever is the strongest) of the casualty, cut the revs, lock over the wheel and accelerate to turn the boat short round, so that you can go slowly back up to him, under control against – say – the wind.

This tactic brings you back up along a line which will be co-incidental with any items likely to have fallen out of the dinghy and are drifting away – bailer, sponge, paddles, clothing and even the rudder on occasions. It will also allow you to station yourself about twenty yards down wind from your subject and to 'play' the gear shift and propeller to keep yourself on station at this safe distance and slightly to the side of him, so that you have an unobstructed view of the crew's efforts to get back upright.

This position and 'play' is important. As already discussed, left to its own devices, the RIB will usually hang tail to the wind, but you need to be bows on to the casualty so that if somebody slips on the centreboard and is injured, or goes over the top of the gunwales and falls into the tangle of ropes and sails, you will immediately see this and can very quickly 'rod' the rescue craft alongside. This is the RIB at its best.

We also have another advantage because most RIB owners have another string to their bow, so they are very often wetsuit (or even drysuit) clad and are not afraid to get into the water to help anyone in difficulty, or to put a bit more weight on the centreboard as it levers the dinghy upright.

Before you assist a crew member or his dinghy, you must always either ask if assistance is required, or wait until they signal you to provide it. Under some sailing rules, any outside hand laid on the competing dinghy, or its occupants, means automatic disqualification.

This is, of course, another reason for being twenty yards off whilst you are standing-by. From a far distant committee boat, your position and your intentions are very clear to interpret. This distance also means that if the dinghy comes upright and is immediately flattened on the other side (a frequent occurrence) it will not fall across yourself. To add the rescue boat to the casualty count really is the height of folly.

If you are asked to assist, the RIB really comes into its own, because it is so easy to manoeuvre into close position and does not cause damage to itself, or to the dinghy if they collide under control. There are several ways you can give help in getting the capsized boat back upright.

The first plan to consider is to get yourself alongside the top of the mast and to pick it up so that it balances across your tube. It may well be that this will create sufficient lift angle for the crew to manage from there. However, if the wind is strong, or if there are any waves, a better plan is to put the rescue boat in gear and drive the dinghy round in a circle until its bows are pointing into the wind. Then when it comes upright again, it is in with a better chance of staying vertical. Even though the rescue boat should be safe from crushing in this position, dinghies have been known to come down again. Thus my own preference is to give the mast a heave and shout "Go!" to my driver, who can then blast us ten yards clear.

If the dinghy requires greater assistance, the RIB can provide it. You can actually stand on the tubes and 'walk' your hands up the dinghy's forestay to lift it upright. If you have gloves, or a piece of rag on board, use them because stainless steel wire stays jumping about in waves can be very unkind to bare flesh.

The big fear and the major problem occurs when the sailing dinghy turns completely turtle so that the top of its mast is pointing straight down to the seabed. The crew's attempts to lever it back up are then hampered by the huge resistance of the mainsail. In the case of a big dinghy like an Albacore, unassisted righting might be impossible.

Prevention being better than cure, if you feel that this situation is going to develop, you can arrest if by tying a spare lifejacket (or a diver's surface marker buoy) to the top of the mast. This will hold the rig horizontal with its sail supported by the water.

For occasions when the worst has happened, we carry a short length of chain which can be made into a loop. If this is put around one of the side shrouds of the upturned dinghy and attached to a light line, it will sink down towards the masthead. The rescue boat is then driven slowly away at right angles, until it is clear enough to tension the line and to start the mast turning back towards the horizontal.

We have only used our short chain in this mode a couple of times, but it has then proved invaluable. But, since having it on board, we have found a number of extra uses for it. This duality also applies to our rescue rope.

Bringing in the casualties

People in the water – even divers – often show a surprising incompetence when they are required to get into a rescue RIB – with its low soft tubes, lifelines, rubber grab handles and stainless steel console rails, surely the easiest of all boats to board. Inevitably, you will have to help them.

Here at the calm of my desk, it seems very easy to manoeuvre our 5.8 metre boat with its gentle giant engine to a place where we can get someone in from the sea. In wind and waves, however, this can prove to be more demanding and less precise than theory indicates. There were a number of early occasions when we were only a few yards from somebody in the water and were pleading that they would swim to us before another wave took us away and we should have to go around again. But they did not.

Accordingly, we now carry about thirty feet of strong, light, floating line attached to a rubber quoit, itself buoyant, which was purchased from a pet shop specialising in dog toys. The ring can be thrown quite accurately and enables us to pull the subject gently to the side of the RIB and to place his hands on the lifeline.

There, it is essential to ask if he is injured, because this would much modify the methods of getting the person into the rescue boat. However, if he is intact, you turn him to face the boat and put his hands on the topside rubber grab handles so that he can pull himself in. If actual assistance is needed two crew members should grip the casualty's shoulders and push him slightly deeper down into the water and immediately bounce him up again. Do this three times to gather upward, buoyant momentum and he will almost propel himself into the boat. Two crew members with a person in a wetsuit, or wearing a lifejacket, can make light work of a heavy body this way. As you push down, the shout is "One! Two! Three! In!" It works.

Towing

Using the RIB as an ocean going tug is seeing it at its worst. The best towing boats are heavy vessels with a long keel well enough down in the water to promote lateral grip and good linear stability and having sufficient mass to 'carry their way' forward. If the tugboat is powered by a big, slow revving engine, so much the better.

Unfortunately, the RIB is the opposite of all those things, but is otherwise such a good rescue boat that it inevitably gets called into tugboat mode. The only thing the skipper can do is to give his boat all possible help.

The problems are the tail of the boat being slewed sideways by a towed boat veering and oscillating off the straight line course. The second is the RIB physically being stopped by the snatch effect of a heavier charge slamming into a wave.

The remedies (in addition to your towing bridle) are to ensure that the tow-line is attached in the very centre of the towed craft. A sailing dinghy's mast is an ideal bollard. Its skipper must be instructed to stay at all times in line with the RIB's wake and to concentrate on staying there. As soon as he veers off to one side, he will give you steering and speed maintenance problems.

The tow-line will probably be yours, so the casualty might need to shorten it up for towing through the harbour and will eventually cast if off. This must be in your mind as you put it on. If possible get your casualty crew to take a couple of turns around a bollard, or the mast and simply to hold on to the free end. There will be no strain on it. The last thing you want is wet rope made fast with a clove hitch. You might not get it off again and could not slip it in a hurry. A round turn and two half hitches is an improvement and a tugboat hitch better still.

Your tow-line should be long (at least 20 metres) and of nylon, or some other rope having a bit of give and stretch to absorb the snatch of a heavy boat. Once you have gently taken up the slack and are under way, you must keep the engine RPM low, especially if the casualty is a weighty one. There is an ever present temptation to give more revs, but this often results in no more than propeller slippage and wasted fuel.

If you are towing with a following sea, low revs make even more sense. Inevitably, the tow surges down a wave in an attempt to overtake the tug. Fortunately the RIB and outboard is such a lively combination that you can accelerate to keep the tow-line taut and even to reposition slightly to correct any small discrepancy in the straight line between the two craft.

Wind surfers

Those board and plank sailers who do it standing up are a feature
of a high proportion of minor rescue incidents. You will be very
lucky to go a whole busy season without getting a wave from one.
(Do you know the code of signals?) After many experiments and
difficulties, we have now entirely given up trying to tow windsurf
boards except to get them clear of surf or rocks. Unless the rig is
stowed and the sailer very competent, you can never prevent the
thing towing 'broadside on'. It takes longer, but it is ultimately
quicker and safer to have the sail properly dismantled and to lift
the entire rig, board and boarder into the rescue boat.

At minimum, take in the sail, wishbone and dagger and put a line
on the very forward point of the board. Its owner should lie
towards its tail and be encouraged to use his streamlined feet in the
water to act as twin rudders. In this way, the towed unit will not
keep burying its nose in waves and can be kept properly in the
RIB's wake.

In calm water, both sailing dinghies and windsurf boards can best
be brought home by lashing them squarely (very squarely)
alongside the RIB. The occupants should still be asked to steer a
parallel course if possible and to assist with the tiller, especially
when the tug is attempting a turn to the side opposite to where the
tow is located. Turning towards him is easy, because he acts like a
paddle, or a side rudder.

Alongside other boats

Because the RIB does not damage either itself or other hulls, it is a
firm favourite as a water taxi. (An owner can earn handsome
money as dedicated runabout to one of the big yachts at an
international regatta.) In some cases of transferring people in
waves, it is more easily accomplished with both vessels making
some way through the water.

Our own current boat, for example, has such an excellent power to weight ratio and such smooth and precise acceleration, that we can hold it on station alongside another boat to a tolerance of about a foot. When the two are parallel and separated by just a couple of inches, the RIB's nose can be turned slightly inwards and held there at a shallow angle until the transfer is complete. Pilot cutters do this as a matter of course. But, if the waves are very big, you need to play things more by ear and circumstance. Rubbing boat fabric against steel hulls or yacht topsides and fittings is not good treatment. You may need to have the bigger boat make a lee for you to shelter behind.

Water skiing

The RIB has not really found favour as a water ski boat for a number of reasons. The first is undoubtedly that its search and rescue image does not exactly coincide with the accepted style of hardware enjoyed and paraded by power-boat clubs. Many skiers also feel that many RIBs are a bit on the light side.

If you are thinking of RIBs less than 4.5 metres in length, this last is justified criticism. I myself have had the amusing experience of cutting hard away from a 3 metre RIB/25 hp outboard combination and exerting so much force that the ski tug almost stopped.

On the other hand, our 5.8/90 hp rig has such fierce acceleration that it will easily simultaneously pull up two ordinary skiers on pairs, or a couple of experts on monos. Once we have either combination up and running on the flats, the RIB copes very well. As a competition or slalom boat, we are not ideal, but for recreational and family skiing, we are a lot of fun.

It is fun which must be tempered with two pieces of advice. The first is to check that your boat insurance does actually include water skiing and its participants and that you are still covered for damage and injury to self and to third parties whilst your boat is engaged in water skiing.

Here we should also launch a plea that you should never have a skier in tow in well populated waters without having someone other than the RIB driver observing the skier and advising whoever is on the wheel. This person can even sit 'the wrong way round' on the central jockey seat to get a good view. The observer observes and the driver drives.

In this way you avoid the sort of happening where a ski boat driver is watching the skier at pull out and either lets his boat go away in a curve across someone else's path or, more likely, fails to see that another boat, obeying the anti collision regulations, has come up quickly and is crossing his bow in the correct manner.

A couple of years back, we were called to the most incredibly stupid search and rescue incident towards dusk of a fine calm evening. A boat with two occupants was towing a skier along the six mile stretch between here and the next harbour. The skier fell off, but he crew were so busy coffee-housing that they did not notice. When they eventually re-engaged their responsibility and back-tracked, they were unable to find him.

Luckily, the chap was wearing a good buoyancy aid and was not injured by his fall, so a search by the entire marine rescue 'cavalry' managed to locate him still in one piece.

As an aside to this, if my partner is driving our own RIB, she can always tell when I fall in because the boat leaps forward. Whether this is a compliment to the fine tuned power of our engine, or a comment on the lumpiness of my inexpert water skiing, is the subject of on-going debate.

Diving

Many of us see the RIB as the perfect dive vehicle. To confess my

The RIB is a perfect dive boat

bias, as a diver I dislike going sub aqua from any other sort of water vehicle and feel very at ease when I know that a RIB with a skipper competent in diver recovery skills is manoeuvring safely to pick me up again.

The requirement is to ensure that the dive coxswain is always in charge of the boat – and not vice versa. We have already discussed the technique of always going either faster or slower than the medium you are travelling in, when we were discussing driving the RIB in waves, but the advice equally applies to strong winds and tidal currents. Being dominated by either means no steerage. In this sense, it is worth practising pointing the nose into a strong current and holding the boat stationary by playing the revs. When you have control, let the nose drop slightly left and the whole boat will move gently sideways in that direction. This is the slalom canoeist's classic ferry glide manoeuvre, which is also a good way of getting safely in to your diver in fast tides. Just glide in elegantly sideways.

I also admit a preference for skippers who think like this in wind and waves. If I have surfaced a bit 'out of puff', the last thing I want is a driver coming bows on at me, determined to bang half a ton of boat onto my head. The bow is, anyway, the part of the boat which goes up and down most, so I do not want to grab hold of an arm jerking lifeline up there.

Better to have the boat come gently up into the eyes of the wind, waves or current, then when it is just beyond the diver in the water, to be turned diagonally in his direction and allowed to drift gently across to him. This means that his first point of contact with the tubes should be just aft of the steering position. This is low and comfortable – even more so if the boat is shielding him from the waves – and where it is easy for the helper to reach out to take a weight belt, or to assist the diver to take off his harness. It does not much matter that the diver's legs generally go under the boat: which is better than trying to swim after a boat moving away on the waves, when you are encumbered with full kit, torch, goody bag, smb and reel.

It is of course common sense to ensure that the engine is either in neutral or switched off to stop the propeller rotating, whilst in close proximity of anyone in the water. This applies to all situations.

Do you know how to pick up divers?

The RIB as a cruising boat

The expression "Bed And Breakfast Cruising" cropped up in our own household almost as a joke and because we were amongst the lucky pioneers of what later became a cult, which was certainly a large part of our own annual RIB programme.

The basic philosophy is that instead of going somewhere slowly and sleeping aboard your chartered yacht, you get there very quickly in the RIB, have more time to enjoy your venue and the greater luxury of a shower and bed and breakfast ashore.

To give an actual example. We currently have a super pacey RIB, but also own 7.5 tonnes of very robust, plodding motor sailer. We also have French friends with a cottage at Tréguier, which is about 125 miles of open sea from here. We visit them in the RIB and the crossing takes a safe five hours. In the motor sailer, a 30 hour crossing would be very acceptable.

Our RIBs have been to the Channel Islands and Normandy, around Scotland, out to St Kilda, across to Ireland around The Fastnet, down to Scillonia and to many places besides. They have all been very memorable controlled adventures.

How you plan your cruise and use your navigation equipment will depend on circumstances, but here suffice it to say that there is not any real possibility of doing serious navigation when you are aboard the boat. All my efforts to use a Breton Plotter, parallel rules, set squares and roller rulers on the boat, even when it is stopped or in harbour, have invariably been frustrated by lack of a flat space to put the chart. A set of dividers to plot distances is about the best you can hope for. This means that all your courses and distances, including all the emergency bolt holes, must be worked out in advance, noted on strong paper and stored in a watertight, transparent folder. We always carry the appropriate charts with us, but recognise the limitations.

You either use ordinary folded charts and accept that you might have to throw them away at the end of the season, or you dig deeper into your pocket for the yachting folding charts printed on waterproof paper which can be written on with erasable chinagraph pens. The ultimate is the totally laminated chart, but this cannot be folded. It can only be carried as a rolled tube.

For such cruising, a demountable navigator/position fixer is ideal. If you can use it at home, either on a 12v car or motor cycle battery, or even fed from a 12v bench supply, it will give you many hours of Winter fun. Our own planning method is to work out all our latitude and longitude waypoints, courses and distances manually, with the dividers and Breton Plotter. This data is then keyed into the Decca, or the GPS receiver in order that its computer side can check all our calculations and vice versa. If we have made an arithmetic mistake, or have pushed a wrong button, the discrepancy between the manually derived and computer produced information immediately shows and can be isolated.

All the cruise details can be left in the navbox's memory, but they are also noted on a piece of paper. Also committed to both an orthodox copy and to the electronic memory are all the positional references for safe havens to which we might run if the weather gets bad and any en route hazards. This back-up information is rarely used, but if a problem does occur, it is comforting to be able to input a hazard and to let the electronics confirm that you are a safe distance from it.

In the same way, it pays to have a ready available note of any buoys or marks close to your route. Then, if you have an electrical problem, or the weather wipes out the Decca, you have a reference point. You could go close to the known mark, or visually estimate your distance from it and use this to give the radio navigation box an approximate position. It will often find itself much more quickly from this than by relying on the auto location software.

This pre-planning should extend to all the data required for entering strange channels and harbours. The RIB travels so quickly, that when you are not in speed restricted space, it is very easy to forget which was the last mark you passed. Poole, Solent and such places as the River Exe all have such areas. St Malo and Tréguier are even worse.

If you have a note of the lat/long and the distinguishing features of a navigation mark, you can soon identify it and re-establish your position after de-orientation, by reference to your notes. If you are going into somewhere like St Malo, write a list of the marks, what they look like and to which side you must leave them. If your crewman ticks off each one as you pass, you should never get lost. There are few sensations worse than running at 20 knots with a fear that a sandbank, or a rock might be in the offing, or even just not knowing exactly where you are. 'Losing the picture' is one of my own worst moments. If it happens, I stop and have a look at the chart, or the list, or both.

Steering on the open sea

About the only navigational problem to taking a RIB cruising so far off-shore that you are out of sight of land is keeping the thing straight. In most cases the driver will be sitting close to the steering compass, which will be tilting and swirling enough to create blinkered vision – that state of mind where you are watching something but not really seeing it. To be 90° off course is not uncommon. The same phenomenon occurs with car drivers in fog, or when you are reading a page which bores you. This does not happen with big slow boats, but RIBs are special.

The obvious way to diminish eye and brain fatigue is by a regular change of helmsman. My personal preference is not to do any more than thirty minutes on the wheel, if the boat is out of sight of land, so there are no reference points of view. Even during this relatively short period of time, you must relieve the eye strain of constant focusing and refocusing as the motion makes your head move in relative position to the compass card. For physiological reasons, as well as those of pilotage, you must look up often and for sufficient time to rest your eyes.

Experienced off-shore RIB coxswains develop a number of ways of keeping the boat on track without being glued to the compass. Small waves are one of the simplest. If they are always striking gently at that point where the tubes curve in to the bow (or similar place) just keep them there and the boat will stay straight.

Occasionally you can steer straight for the sun, or it will cause the shadow of a console grab rail to fall across a particular point on the console, or to align with a name on a tube. By keeping shadow and fixed point in constant relative alignment, you will know that the boat's head is not wandering. I have also steered at clouds for two or three minutes at a time without getting off track.

It very often happens that you see the funnel of a ship on a distant horizon. It angle of travel will be changing so slowly in relation to your own line of travel that it can make a good steering reference. You rest you eyes by telling yourself to "steer just to the left of the funnel" for five minutes or so.

All these tricks of the trade just make life more secure and easier. Fortunately, RIBs are safe and even if not always easy they are always exciting. As fast cruising, rescue and general messing about boats, they have more going for them than anything else I have ever driven.

Chapter Eleven

Service and maintenance

Over the twenty years of my association with 'rubber' boats, a noticeable – and very welcome trend – has been a massive reduction in the amount of time and cash swallowed up by repair, maintenance and routine servicing of both boat and engine.

There are a dozen reasons for this, but they are all under the umbrella of 'the improvements created by progress' – better engines, better malleable materials and the arrival of the RIB, which removed from my life the vexations of perforated, lace-like rubber floors, irritating tiny pin-prick holes and gravel in the tube-to-floor V slot.

The RIB is even kinder to lazy owners. Ours gets nothing more than a very regular hosing down with fresh water as often as possible during the season and then gets a big treatment during the 'bedding' process before its annual five month Winter storage.

Firstly, we are quite meticulous about washing down every square millimetre of fabric with a reasonably strong cocktail of warm water and ordinary washing up liquid. Once this has been hosed off, we go round again to check for persistent blemishes, which might be grease, tar, chewing gum or seaweed stains. A warm cloth and neat domestic detergent applied with a bit of extra pressure on the cloth generally does the trick. Only rarely have we resorted to very, very careful use of petrol, lighter fuel or surgical spirit.

Boat materials are highly resistant to such solvents, but it is still prudent to mask the area off with adhesive tape. This tolerance – and the cleaning process as a whole – is applicable to both the traditional neoprene/Hypalon formulae and to polyurethane material.

The inside of the hull is treated in much the same way. It is a task of plenty of flushing water and plenty of elbow grease on particular spots in between. Such areas as the non-slip floor can only really be done with a scrubbing brush.

For this inside job, you need to get the nose of the boat blocked up as high as possible in order to create a water flow to the self drainers. The most important job is to get out all the sand and abrasive grit. If you have access to a steam cleaner, this is even better and a good nozzle will get you right inside the seats and lockers.

There are always some spaces where water collects and refuses to run back to the drains. It is a mistake to leave it, so wise owners have some soak-up rags and a bucket and sponge on site. Even with the best of my RIBs, I have never owned a sealed hull which did not at some time let in a few drops of water.

If you have the sort of hull which is designed to let it in (eg the Avon Searider flooding hull) you will need to rinse out the interior with a very strong detergent mix and possibly add an algicide. Green fungus will grow in any water which is left standing. You would also be advised to dry this space rapidly and thoroughly.

The most objectionable RIB hull I have ever examined was a foreign flooding hull model which had been left afloat for a year in a marina. The level of weed and mollusc growth inside the GRP hull was quite startling. When it began to dry out, the smell it created evinced a number of adjectives from the people working on it and startling was far and away the mildest.

A sealed hull takes in small amounts of seepage water through the screw and bolt holes which secure the fixings. Even though they will have been backed up with silicone at installation, this compound stiffens and peels with age and with the microscopic, but violent, amount of flexing and shock wave impact which a RIB is forced to endure in its normal life at sea and on the road trailer. Inevitably these holes permit small amounts of water to ingress.

If you shake your boat on the trailer and can hear a quantity of water swishing about inside, you had best let it out. About the only way is to create the maximum possible bow to stern down-slope and to drill two very precisely positioned holes in the transom.

Where you place the drill is very important. If you go into any of the fore and aft floor supports or transom bracing knees, the holes will not work. You need to get them as low as possible without drilling into the lower moulding. Some precise measurements are needed, even in consultation with the boat's builder, to get it right. Two holes (about 5 mm is enough) are needed to get an adequate water out, air in flow.

You may have to leave the boat 'a-slope' for a couple of days to be sure that she is really dry, but when you are quite sure that the hull is empty, a dab of flexible sealant and a well cut rubber bung hammered back into place, should settle things for at least another couple of years.

In addition to floor fixings, ski rings and bow eyes work loose and can be a source of water ingress. It is for this reason that I have never been an admirer of towing/mooring eyes whose internal fastenings are inside a sealed hull. After a couple of years, they always vibrate into looseness. So, the only possible treatment is to back off the nuts, ease the plates, clean the area and re-tighten the ensemble onto a new pad of proprietary marine sealant. At re-assembly, it might also pay to give the threads a touch of Loctite (or similar) and even to add a locking nut.

If you are towed, or use the eye as an anchor tie off, this U-bolt is put under a vast amount of twisting pressure – even before you use it to pull the boat hard down into the trailer snubber, so it is not surprising that it needs a little periodic maintenance.

The outside of the hull is no different from any other GRP assembly. The wise owner, ie a person who does not let the waves ground and pound his boat on shingle beaches, or tries to drag it over abrasive sand, will have zero maintenance. If you treat your boat as though its bottom is as vulnerable as that of a straight inflatable, you will do its health and appearance no harm and you will be offering your pocket a favour.

The other source of GRP nicks and scratches is the trailer. There are occasions when the boat jumps off the rubber keel rollers and is struck by their metal supports and a failure to centralise the hull on its side rails and then to 'sweat' it down into total trailer immobility will also cause GRP damage.

In this respect, trailer straps thrown over the tubes have a less than perfect reputation, because they allow the boat to bounce and wobble on rough roads. To avoid damage, there is nothing to beat ropes and spliced eyes made fast to rigid parts of the boat and firm parts of the trailer.

If you need to patch up gelcoat, by far the simplest way of getting a good colour match is to go back to the boat's builder to make some enquiries about the exact pigments he uses. Most of the smaller companies are very good about this and will generally let you have a small quantity to mix in with your resin.

A couple of scratches apart, I have never needed to do anything other than wash the outside of my RIB's hull, although the racing fraternity occasionally turn the boat upside down and treat the hull to a coat of Winter wax polish and a light machine buffing in Spring.

Tube maintenance

Because of the high quality of the components RIB tubes are also trouble-free, especially if you are always careful to keep them up to good pressure. Here it should be remembered that what an owner sees as a leak because a tube feels 'squidgy', might be no more than the air inside contracting as the temperature drops. If you suspect an air leak, the source could be any of three.

Valves

Valves rarely need servicing if the cap is always kept firmly in place. If you are lax about this a deposit of salt builds up on the sealing flange and this can cause a very slow leak which can only be cured with warm fresh water and a very small brush.

A valve failure is a rarity. If it happens you will need professional solvents to remove the old and professional adhesives to bond in the new. One owner we met solved the replacement problem by cutting out a six inch diameter circle from his tube and fitting the valve in whilst this was flat, then re-inserting it as a patch. It never worked really well and always looked dreadful. He would have been better advised – as we all are – to swallow our pride by taking major valve tasks back to the boat's maker, or his recommended local agent.

Holes

Small holes of pin prick size are also rare and when they do occur can be the devil to locate. About the best way is to wipe the suspect area with a strong mix of washing up liquid and water, then watch for the bubbles. As soon as you see a tell-tale mark the spot with a small circle in biro. This will still be visible when you wipe the area dry.

I confess that I have repaired very small holes in inflatable tubes with nothing more than a very careful, very gentle, very small touch with a soldering iron. It is, however, more usual to put on a patch from the maker's repair kit, which should be supplied as standard with every boat.

When you have selected a patch of appropriate size to cover the tear with an adequate amount of overlap, hold the patch in place and draw round it with a biro. if you are cutting your own patch, a circle will stay attached much better than a piece of rubber with corners.

From there on, it is a case of following the repair kit's instructions about the number of coats, the drying time for the patch to be safe and the curing time before the bond is strong enough to withstand pressure. In all patching, haste and lack of patience are the chief cause of poor workmanship and poor sealing.

Seam tapes

Seam tapes are one of the most difficult parts of RIB tube construction. Nowadays, most of the joins needed to convert a flat sheet of material into a sausage (or even more complex to shape a bow) are cut on a mitre, or overlapped, then seam taped both inside and out.

For an owner, the irritant occurs when the boat has had a few outings and he might discover that one edge of a seam tape is beginning to lift. The seam is probably not wicking air, but the delamination looks scruffy. One problem of getting tapes to stick is that of difficulty in applying bonding pressure to a curved, air-filled surface. The other is that in order to get the narrow tape to stick right across its width, the adhesive needs to be applied to (more than) its width. If it remains outside the tape line, it looks very untidy when it dries.

Here we have another case for drawing a few lines and some very careful application of masking tape. Again, as a heretic out in the field, I have actually repaired a lifting seam with one-shot instant glue from a seaside supermarket.

Only on one occasion have I been involved in seam tape refurbishment which was so bad that more drastic measures were needed. One edge of the tape had lifted of its own accord and then been even further pulled from the tube by some bored children. The point of no return was reached when a diver going over the side caught his crab hook in the lifted portion and stretched it so badly that a splice was necessary. We stripped back a generous length with the aid of a whole mountain of patience plus some adhesive solvent provided by the boat's builder, before making a couple of diagonal cuts to remove the old tape. The space to be occupied by the new was masked and the first coat of adhesive applied, then left to dry and await the second.

The actual tape was put on by winding an over-length strip as a spiral onto a beer can. It could then be coated up without mess, distortion or sticking to itself. When the adhesive had 'gone off' to tackiness, the can and tape were tautly rolled down the line of the seam by one pair of hands and equally carefully pressed into place by an assistant, who also cut the mitre when the end of the run was reached.

Outboards

Outboard motors are certainly no longer outside the amateur's maintenance competence. We have passed beyond that age where fiddly magnetos and breaker points needed to be adjusted. Generally speaking, capacitor discharge ignition either works, or the engineer replaces the module with a new one.

Beyond this, engine care is a matter of reading the handbook and applying some common sense to its recommendations. However, before we interpret these, let us prick your conscience with a cautionary tale.

One of my own engines, which I had run for five very successful, but very carefully maintained years, was a semi waterproofed model, built on a two cylinder and piston assembly block which was so well thought of that three of the major outboard manufacturers were using it. In fact it is still in production in only slightly modified form today.

It was properly Winterised and sold on with the boat in late November. I was sorry to see it go and even sorrier to hear the following May that it had blown up on its new owner. The story would appear to be that in the excitement of acquisition, the engine had been fired up for a quick test at the new owner's house and (apparently)with no cooling water supply in situ. It had also been given a quick trip down the estuary and then left in the garden to wait for the new season.

The allegory contains all the elements of how not to treat an outboard – overheat, running with no cooling and revved hard with no load on the prop and crankshaft, then left for a number of months with no protection and with an amount of salt water in the system. All good cracking and corrosive factors.

Winterising the engine

When the outboard is to be left unused for any period longer than – say – six weeks, especially in a harsh, cold climate, it should be properly stored.

The first step is a twenty minute run at 20% power with a generous supply of fresh water running through the cooling system. There are two equally good ways of doing this, if you do not have access to a marine engineer's test tank.

You can drop the engine's cooling water intake down into a tank of your own making – a dustbin, a cut down oil drum, or even a redundant domestic cold water header tank. If this is on the small side, the under water exhaust will soon pollute the contents and cause a film of sooty scum to gather on the surface. The remedy is a slow running hosepipe feed of fresh water.

The tank is a bit clumsy with an engine bolted through the transom, but it does work and has the advantage that you can add a proper engine cooling system detergent to the water as it is pulled in.

Some engines have a screw-in plug with an adaptor to attach a hose straight into the cooling system.

The more usual amateur method is with a set of rubber 'earphones' attached to a hosepipe delivering a good, strong supply of fresh water. Earphones can be purchased from any outboard engineer and should be a standard item in every outboard motor owner's tool box. They clamp over the cooling water intakes below the anti cavitation plate and let the water in under sealed pressure.

As the engine's cooling pipes are being descaled and cleaned by this process, it is not a bad idea to run some proprietary engine cleaner through the hot parts. This compound comes as an aerosol and is inserted by squirting in via the carburettor air intakes.

Stage Two is to let this clear, then squirt in one of the good quality engine storage and sealing mixes. This again is an aerosol injected by the same method. Its purpose is to give all the moving internal parts a good coat of the sort of lubricant which will stay protectively in place for the duration of idleness.

(More outboard motor damage is caused by lack of use than ever happened from daily employment.)

During this process, which will take about five minutes of alternately squirting into each carb in turn, the engine will give off white and grey smoke in fairly liberal amounts. When it begins to run slightly rough and even to cough a bit, the task is nearly completed and should be continued until the engine literally chokes itself into stillness.

Experienced engineers can gauge this well enough to be able to remove the fuel feed so that the engine runs out of petrol at the same time that it dies of storage seal benefits.

This stage is completed by disconnecting the earphones and also uncoupling the ignition leads before taking out the sparking plugs. Most engines have the facility for cord and manual start, which will slowly revolve the flywheel to expel any last dregs of water and allow you simultaneously to squirt the last of your storage seal in through the plug holes. The spark plug apertures themselves can be given a squirt of water dispersant and the plugs replaced. Before you put them back, give them a clean up with a drop of petrol and a small wire brush. You can then start your engine up again with these old plugs on line next season and let them burn off the storage seal, but replace them with new plugs before your first outing.

Now it is the time to take apart and clean the fuel filter bowl, grease all the connecting rods and cables, clean away any dirt and grease, check all the wire connectors and give the whole engine a birthday of water repellent aerosol before replacing the cover.

If you have the normal remote fuel tank supplied with an outboard, you must either completely fill it with neat petrol, or empty it and leave it open in a very warm dry place. The same applies to an in-built stainless steel tank – fill or empty.

A frequent cause of early season outboard failure is sediment slowly sinking into the bottom of the tank and getting into the jets. This is even more frequent amongst owners who use pre-mixed two stroke petroil cocktails. There is no reason why you should not use last year's petrol (or petroil) in your car by adding quantities in with fresh petrol. The lubricant additive will certainly do it no harm.

However, new season, new petrol, new oil and new gear case lube should be the rule.

Some owners do not change the gear case oil at the end of the season. A personal preference is to do so in order to examine the old for discolouration, which implies water and a leaking oil seal or – worse – any bits of metal caused by grinding gears. This way, you do at least have all Winter to solve the problems.

The prudent change the lower case lube at the end of the season and again after about three or four hours of the new.

The final Winter bye-bye is a thorough clean of the outside and a spray of WD40 or similar, followed by removal of the prop for safe keeping and service and to ensure that you give the splines a new coat of grease and a new split pin before you go to sea again.

Winterising is almost simpler to do than to describe. The whole boat and engine process will take no more than a morning – say a day including the drying time. It might be a chore, but the savings in deterioration and renovation costs are huge in proportion – and that is even before you add in the safety factors involved.

The pillion is not really driving!

Chapter Twelve

The Last Words

So, where do we go from here? The RIB is not immune from the normal courses of history. Most human endeavours follow the pendulum principle. Experiments, and the perpetual chase for eye catching, money making novelty moves the activity ever further away from its original concepts, then when it has reached a ridiculously way-out level, sense and economics take over again and regulate a return to the pendulum's centre point.

This constantly repeating scenario is most often seen in the World of clothing. The wide skirt got to be so broad that special doors and staircases were built just to accommodate the crinoline. This was followed by a reactionary period of very slim costume. More recent times have seen the female hemline yo-yoing between the extremes of the micro skirt and the maxi, but repeatedly settling in the middle.

The RIB is at a development state where the pendulum does not have too much further to go. Because a combination of soft tops and hard bottoms is so versatile and safe, plenty of people have tried to use it in ways very different from the original Atlantic College concepts. Quite often they have produced some really crazy boats.

In Europe, a small but influential cabal have become very enthusiastic about racing and this activity's devotees have produced some very weird designs which travel very fast, but are a long way removed from the basic balance between speed and stability. Other fans of multi-hull boats, cathedral hulls and building in aluminium have also produced mavericks. It is not clear whether their motives have been to improve their own boat type, or to bring what they see as a better hull form to the RIB. The most common incentive however, has been the desire to make money. The most common result has been failure.

Almost airborn

Collective noun for RIBS – an 'Air' perhaps?

Amidst all this activity the basic deep V hull, with various degrees of deadrise, has survived. This was and still is inevitable. Seafarers are a very conservative group. They like what works well and what hangs together for a long time no matter how it is treated. Because their lives depend on the boat, proper seamen are much more impressed by history and experience than by novelty.

This slow evolution does not reject progress. It took the present group of hull shapes a long time to evolve. These fundamental designs then remain relatively unaltered, but improvements are made in strength, materials and methods of construction. The shift from wood to the vastly superior qualities of GRP is a classic example of this progress.

The RIB is set to follow the same course. We have seen them built far too big, far too wide, much too heavy, much too long and much too expensive, which is very far removed from the initial concept of a portable (towable) fast load carrier.

So, the pendulum is swinging back towards the centre of finance and sanity, but this does not imply regression. There is still plenty of development work going on to improve the RIB. Kevlar and other very light, very strong materials down below and high frequency welding up top are just two areas which people are working on. We also have plenty of electronics now being designed with open boats in mind and when you see the pay-roll length of Japanese outboard manufacturers' research and development departments, you realise that there is still plenty more to come.

All this puts both the buyer and the builder in very good positions. The former knows that there is a strong and growing market for good products. The prospective owner is certain to be able to get the sort of boat he wants from one of the excellent companies looking for business.

There are many arguments in favour of buying a production line boat and engine package, with a few electronic pieces thrown in for luck.

Equally, the RIB is very convenient for customising and this should not cost anything extra if you know what you want your boat for and what you want in it and on it. As long as the builder knows right from day one, he can configure your model to suit. He has to add all the bits to the basic mould anyway, so he may as well do it to your requirements.

However, make sure that you get it right. Owning a RIB is not a mere flirtation. The best of them are so tough and so long lasting that a betrothal is certain. Once you have driven your first, you never lose the thrill, so a life long marriage is also on the cards.

If yours gets to be as good as my life with the RIB has been in the past and continues to be, even after a long and busy association, you are letting yourself in for a lot of fun.

– and finally, a standing start

Index